I0007259

Amazon WorkSpaces Administration Guide

A catalogue record for this book is available from the Hong Kong Public Libraries.

Published in Hong Kong by Samurai Media Limited.

Email: info@samuraimedia.org

ISBN 9789888408641

Copyright 2018 Amazon Web Services, Inc. and/or its affiliates.
Minor modifications for publication Copyright 2018 Samurai Media Limited.

This book is licensed under the Creative Commons Attribution-ShareAlike 4.0 International Public License.

Background Cover Image by https://www.flickr.com/people/webtreatsetc/

Contents

What Is Amazon WorkSpaces? 7
Features 7
Architecture 7
Accessing Your WorkSpace 8
Pricing 8
How to Get Started 9

Get Started with Amazon WorkSpaces Quick Setup 10
Before You Begin 10
Step 1: Launch the WorkSpace 10
Step 2: Connect to the WorkSpace 12
Step 3: Clean Up (Optional) 13

Networking, Access, and Security for Amazon WorkSpaces 15

Configure a VPC for Amazon WorkSpaces 16
Step 1: Allocate an Elastic IP Address 17
Step 2: Create a VPC 18
Step 3: Add a Subnet 18
Step 4: Verify the Route Tables 19

Port Requirements for Amazon WorkSpaces 20
Ports for Client Applications 20
Ports for Web Access 20
Whitelisted Domains and Ports 21
PCoIP Gateway and Health Check Servers 21
Network Interfaces 22
    Management Interface IP Ranges 22
    Management Interface Ports 23
    Primary Interface Ports 23

Amazon WorkSpaces Client Network Requirements 24

Control Access to Amazon WorkSpaces Resources 25
Specifying Amazon WorkSpaces Resources in an IAM Policy 27
    WorkSpace ARN 27
    Bundle ARN 28
    API Actions with No Support for Resource-Level Permissions 28

Restrict WorkSpaces Access to Trusted Devices 29
Step 1: Create the Certificates 29
Step 2: Deploy Client Certificates to the Trusted Devices 29
Step 3: Configure the Restriction 29

Provide Internet Access from Your WorkSpace 31
Manually Assign IP Addresses 31

Security Groups for Your WorkSpaces 32

IP Access Control Groups for Your WorkSpaces 33
Create an IP Access Control Group 33
Associate an IP Access Control Group with a Directory 33
Copy an IP Access Control Group 33

Delete an IP Access Control Group 34

Set Up PCoIP Zero Client for WorkSpaces   **35**

Manage Directories for Amazon WorkSpaces   **36**

Register a Directory with Amazon WorkSpaces   **37**

Update Directory Details for Your WorkSpaces   **38**
Select an Organizational Unit 38
Configure Automatic IP Addresses 39
Control Device Access 39
Manage Local Administrator Permissions 39
Update the AD Connector Account (AD Connector) 40
Multi-factor Authentication (AD Connector) 40

Delete the Directory for Your WorkSpaces   **42**

Set Up Active Directory Administration Tools for Amazon WorkSpaces   **43**

Manage Your WorkSpaces Using Group Policy   **45**
Install the Group Policy Administrative Template 45
Local Printer Support 46
Clipboard Redirection 46
Setting the Session Resume Timeout 47

Launch a Virtual Desktop Using Amazon WorkSpaces   **48**

Launch a WorkSpace Using Microsoft AD   **49**
Before You Begin 49
Step 1: Create a Microsoft AD Directory 49
Step 2: Create a WorkSpace 50
Step 3: Connect to the WorkSpace 50
Next Steps 51

Launch a WorkSpace Using Simple AD   **52**
Before You Begin 52
Step 1: Create a Simple AD Directory 52
Step 2: Create a WorkSpace 53
Step 3: Connect to the WorkSpace 54
Next Steps 54

Launch a WorkSpace Using AD Connector   **55**
Before You Begin 55
Step 1: Create an AD Connector 55
Step 2: Create a WorkSpace 56
Step 3: Connect to the WorkSpace 57
Next Steps 57

Launch a WorkSpace Using a Trusted Domain   **58**
Before You Begin 58
Step 1: Establish a Trust Relationship 58
Step 2: Create a WorkSpace 58
Step 3: Connect to the WorkSpace 59
Next Steps 59

Administer Your WorkSpaces   **60**

Manage WorkSpaces Users   **61**
     Edit User Information 61
     Send an Invitation Email 61

Manage the WorkSpace Running Mode   **62**
     Modify the Running Mode 62
     Stop and Start an AutoStop WorkSpace 62
     Set Maintenance Mode 63

Modify a WorkSpace   **64**

Tag a WorkSpace   **65**

Encrypt a WorkSpace   **66**
     Prerequisites 66
     Limits 66
     Encrypting WorkSpaces 66
     Viewing Encrypted WorkSpaces 66
     IAM Permissions and Roles for Encryption 67

Reboot a WorkSpace   **69**

Rebuild a WorkSpace   **70**

Delete a WorkSpace   **71**

Upgrade Windows 10 BYOL WorkSpaces   **72**
     Known Limitations 73
     Troubleshooting 73
     Update Your WorkSpace Registry Using a PowerShell Script 73

WorkSpace Bundles and Images   **75**

Create a Custom WorkSpaces Bundle   **76**

Update a Custom WorkSpaces Bundle   **78**

Delete a Custom WorkSpaces Bundle   **79**

Bring Your Own Windows Desktop Images   **80**
     Requirements 80
     Getting Started 80

Monitoring Amazon WorkSpaces   **81**
     Amazon WorkSpaces Metrics 81
     Dimensions for Amazon WorkSpaces Metrics 82
     Monitoring Example 83

Troubleshooting Amazon WorkSpaces Issues   **85**
     Launching WorkSpaces in my connected directory often fails 85
     Launching WorkSpaces fails with an internal error 85
     Can't connect to a WorkSpace with an interactive logon banner 85
     No WorkSpaces in my directory can connect to the Internet 85
     I receive a "DNS unavailable" error when I try to connect to my on-premises directory 85
     I receive a "Connectivity issues detected" error when I try to connect to my on-premises directory . . 86
     I receive an "SRV record" error when I try to connect to my on-premises directory 86
     One of my WorkSpaces has a state of "Unhealthy" 86

The state of my apps was not saved when my WorkSpace was stopped 87

Amazon WorkSpaces Limits 88

Document History 89

What Is Amazon WorkSpaces?

Amazon WorkSpaces enables you to provision virtual, cloud-based Microsoft Windows desktops for your users, known as *WorkSpaces*. Amazon WorkSpaces eliminates the need to procure and deploy hardware or install complex software. You can quickly add or remove users as your needs change. Users can access their virtual desktops from multiple devices or web browsers.

For more information, see Amazon WorkSpaces.

Features

- Select from a range of hardware configurations, software configurations, and AWS regions. For more information, see Amazon WorkSpaces Bundles.
- Connect to your WorkSpace and pick up from right where you left off. Amazon WorkSpaces provides a persistent desktop experience.
- Amazon WorkSpaces provides the flexibility of either monthly or hourly billing for WorkSpaces. For more information, see Amazon WorkSpaces Pricing.
- Deploy and manage applications for your WorkSpaces using Amazon WorkSpaces Application Manager (Amazon WAM).
- Bring your own licenses and applications, or purchase them from the AWS Marketplace for Desktop Apps.
- Create a standalone managed directory for your users, or connect your WorkSpaces to your on-premises directory so that your users can use their existing credentials to obtain seamless access to corporate resources.
- Use the same tools to manage WorkSpaces that you use to manage on-premises desktops.
- Use multi-factor authentication (MFA) for additional security.
- Use AWS Key Management Service (AWS KMS) to encrypt data at rest, disk I/O, and volume snapshots.

Architecture

Each WorkSpace is associated with the virtual private cloud (VPC), and a directory to store and manage information for your WorkSpaces and users. Directories are managed through the AWS Directory Service, which offers the following options: Simple AD, AD Connector, or AWS Directory Service for Microsoft Active Directory (Enterprise Edition), also known as Microsoft AD. For more information, see the AWS Directory Service Administration Guide.

Amazon WorkSpaces uses a directory, either AWS Directory Service or Microsoft AD, to authenticate users. Users access their WorkSpaces using a client application from a supported device or a web browser and log in using their directory credentials. The login information is sent to an authentication gateway, which forwards the traffic to the directory for the WorkSpace. After the user is authenticated, streaming traffic is initiated through the streaming gateway.

Client applications use HTTPS over port 443 for all authentication and session-related information. Client applications uses port 4172 for pixel streaming to the WorkSpace and for network health checks. For more information, see Ports for Client Applications.

Each WorkSpace has two elastic network interfaces (ENI) associated with it: an ENI for management and streaming (eth0) and a primary ENI (eth1). The primary ENI has an IP address provided by your VPC, from the same subnets used by the directory. This ensures that traffic from your WorkSpace can easily reach the directory. Access to resources in the VPC is controlled by the security groups assigned to the primary ENI. For more information, see Network Interfaces.

The following diagram shows the architecture of Amazon WorkSpaces.

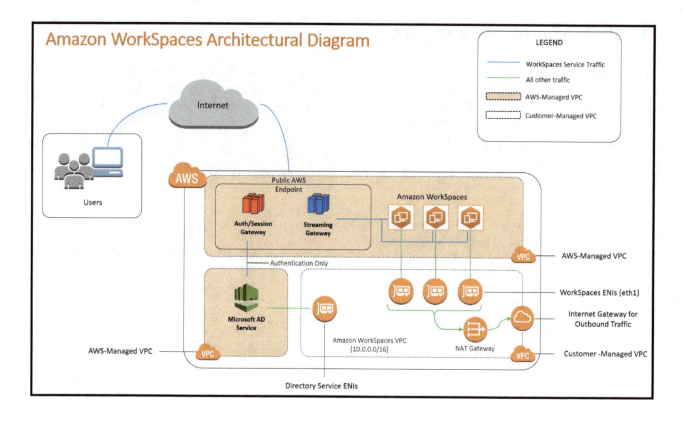

Accessing Your WorkSpace

You can connect to your WorkSpaces using the client application for a supported device or using a supported web browser on a supported operating system.

There are client applications for the following devices:

- Windows computers
- Mac computers
- Chromebooks
- iPads
- Android tablets
- Fire tablets
- Zero client devices

The following web browsers are supported on Windows, macOS, and Linux:

- Chrome 53 and later
- Firefox 49 and later

For more information, see Amazon WorkSpaces Clients in the *Amazon WorkSpaces User Guide.*

Pricing

After you sign up for AWS, you can get started with Amazon WorkSpaces for free using the Amazon WorkSpaces free tier offer. For more information, see Amazon WorkSpaces Pricing.

With Amazon WorkSpaces, you pay only for what you use. You are charged based on the bundle and the number of WorkSpaces that you launch. The pricing for Amazon WorkSpaces includes the use of Simple AD and AD Connector but not the use of Microsoft AD.

Amazon WorkSpaces provides monthly or hourly billing for WorkSpaces. With monthly billing, you pay a fixed fee for unlimited usage, which is best for users who use their WorkSpaces full time. With hourly billing, you pay a small fixed monthly fee per WorkSpace, plus a low hourly rate for each hour the WorkSpace is running. For more information, see Amazon WorkSpaces Pricing.

How to Get Started

To create a WorkSpace, try one of the following tutorials:

- Get Started with Amazon WorkSpaces Quick Setup
- Launch a WorkSpace Using Microsoft AD
- Launch a WorkSpace Using Simple AD
- Launch a WorkSpace Using AD Connector
- Launch a WorkSpace Using a Trusted Domain

Get Started with Amazon WorkSpaces Quick Setup

In this tutorial, you'll learn how to provision a virtual, cloud-based Microsoft Windows desktop, known as a *WorkSpace*, using Amazon WorkSpaces and AWS Directory Service.

This tutorial uses the Quick Setup option to launch your WorkSpace. This option is available only if you have never launched a WorkSpace.

Note

Quick Setup is not supported in the EU (Frankfurt) region.

Alternatively, see Launch a Virtual Desktop Using Amazon WorkSpaces.

Topics

- Before You Begin
- Step 1: Launch the WorkSpace
- Step 2: Connect to the WorkSpace
- Step 3: Clean Up (Optional)

Before You Begin

- You must have an AWS account to create or administer a WorkSpace. Users do not need an AWS account to connect to and use their WorkSpaces.
- When you launch a WorkSpace, you must select a WorkSpace bundle. For more information, see Amazon WorkSpaces Bundles.
- When you launch a WorkSpace, you must specify profile information for the user, including a username and email address. The user completes their profile by specifying a password. Information about WorkSpaces and users is stored in a directory.
- Amazon WorkSpaces is not available in every region. Verify the supported regions and select a region for your WorkSpaces. For more information about the supported regions, see Amazon WorkSpaces Pricing by AWS Region.

Step 1: Launch the WorkSpace

Using Quick Setup, you can launch your first WorkSpace in minutes.

To launch a WorkSpace

1. Open the Amazon WorkSpaces console at https://console.aws.amazon.com/workspaces/.

2. Choose **Get Started Now**.

3. On the **Get Started with Amazon WorkSpaces** page, next to **Quick Setup**, choose **Launch**.

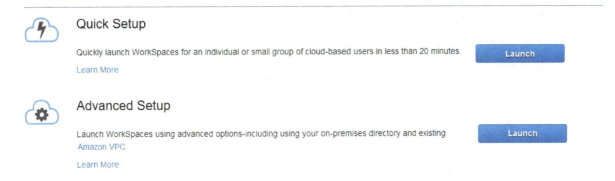

Get Started with Amazon WorkSpaces

Choose an option below to set up your WorkSpaces.

Quick Setup

Quickly launch WorkSpaces for an individual or small group of cloud-based users in less than 20 minutes.
Learn More

Launch

Advanced Setup

Launch WorkSpaces using advanced options-including using your on-premises directory and existing Amazon VPC.
Learn More

Launch

Cancel

4. For **Bundles**, select a bundle for the user.

Bundle	CPU	Memory	Storage
Standard with Windows 7 `Free tier eligible`	2 vCPU	4 GiB	50 GB
Standard with Windows 10 `Free tier eligible`	2 vCPU	4 GiB	50 GB
Standard with Windows 7 and Office 2010	2 vCPU	4 GiB	50 GB
Standard with Windows 7 and Office 2013	2 vCPU	4 GiB	50 GB
Standard with Windows 10 and Office 2016	2 vCPU	4 GiB	50 GB
Performance with Windows 7	2 vCPU	7.5 GiB	100 GB
Performance with Windows 10	2 vCPU	7.5 GiB	100 GB
Performance with Windows 7 and Office 2010	2 vCPU	7.5 GiB	100 GB

5. For **Enter User Details**, complete **Username**, **First Name**, **Last Name**, and **Email**.

Enter User Details

Username	First Name	Last Name	Email
johnd	John	Doe	johnd@mycompany.com

6. Choose **Launch WorkSpaces**.

7. On the confirmation page, choose **View the WorkSpaces Console**. The initial status of the WorkSpace is PENDING. When the launch is complete, the status is AVAILABLE and an invitation is sent to the email address that you specified for the user.

Quick Setup

Quick Setup completes the following tasks on your behalf:

- Creates an IAM role to allow the Amazon WorkSpaces service to create elastic network interfaces and list your Amazon WorkSpaces directories. This role has the name `workspaces_DefaultRole`.
- Creates a virtual private cloud (VPC).
- Sets up a Simple AD directory in the VPC that is used to store user and WorkSpace information. The directory has an administrator account and it is enabled for Amazon WorkDocs.
- Creates the specified user accounts and adds them to the directory.
- Creates WorkSpace instances. Each WorkSpace receives a public IP address to provide Internet access. The running mode is AlwaysOn. For more information, see Manage the WorkSpace Running Mode.
- Sends invitation emails to the specified users.

Step 2: Connect to the WorkSpace

After you receive the invitation email, you can connect to the WorkSpace using the client of your choice. After you sign in, the client displays the WorkSpace desktop.

To connect to the WorkSpace

1. If you haven't set up credentials for the user already, open the link in the invitation email and follow the directions. Remember the password that you specify as you will need it to connect to your WorkSpace.

   Note that passwords are case-sensitive and must be between 8 and 64 characters in length, inclusive. Passwords must contain at least one character from three of the following categories: lowercase letters (a-z), uppercase letters (A-Z), numbers (0-9), and the set ~!@#$%^&*_-+=`|\(){}[]:;"'<>,.?/.

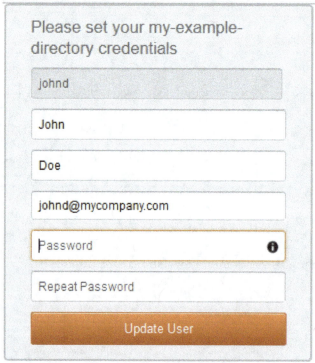

2. When prompted, download one of the client applications or launch Web Access. For more information about the requirements for each client, see Amazon WorkSpaces Clients in the *Amazon WorkSpaces User Guide*.

   If you aren't prompted and you haven't installed a client application already, open https://clients.amazon-workspaces.com and follow the directions.

3. Start the client, enter the registration code from the invitation email, and choose **Register**.

4. When prompted to sign in, type the username and password, and then choose **Sign In**.

5. (Optional) When prompted to save your credentials, choose **Yes**.

Step 3: Clean Up (Optional)

If you are finished with the WorkSpace that you created for this tutorial, you can delete it.

To delete the WorkSpace

1. Open the Amazon WorkSpaces console at https://console.aws.amazon.com/workspaces/.

2. In the navigation pane, choose **WorkSpaces**.

3. Select your WorkSpace and choose **Actions**, **Remove WorkSpaces**.

4. When prompted for confirmation, choose **Remove WorkSpaces**.

5. (Optional) If you are not using the directory with another application, such as Amazon WorkDocs, Amazon WorkMail, or Amazon Chime, you can delete it as follows:

   1. In the navigation pane, choose **Directories**.

   2. Select your directory and choose **Actions**, **Deregister**.

   3. Select your directory again and choose **Actions**, **Delete**.

   4. When prompted for confirmation, choose **Delete**.

Networking, Access, and Security for Amazon WorkSpaces

As a WorkSpace administrator, you must understand the following about Amazon WorkSpaces networking and security.

Topics

- Configure a VPC for Amazon WorkSpaces
- Port Requirements for Amazon WorkSpaces
- Amazon WorkSpaces Client Network Requirements
- Control Access to Amazon WorkSpaces Resources
- Restrict WorkSpaces Access to Trusted Devices
- Provide Internet Access from Your WorkSpace
- Security Groups for Your WorkSpaces
- IP Access Control Groups for Your WorkSpaces
- Set Up PCoIP Zero Client for WorkSpaces

Configure a VPC for Amazon WorkSpaces

Amazon WorkSpaces launches your WorkSpaces in a virtual private cloud (VPC). If you use AWS Directory Service to create a Microsoft AD or a Simple AD, we recommend that you configure the VPC with one public subnet and two private subnets. Configure your directory to launch your WorkSpaces in the private subnets.

Note that you can associate an IPv6 CIDR block with your VPC and subnets. However, if you configure your subnets to automatically assign IPv6 addresses to instances launched in the subnet, then you cannot launch WorkSpaces using the Performance or Graphics bundles. By default, this setting is disabled. To check this setting, open the Amazon VPC console, select your subnet, and choose **Subnet Actions**, **Modify auto-assign IP settings**.

To provide Internet Access to WorkSpaces in a private subnet, configure a NAT gateway in the public subnet. For alternative methods of providing Internet access for your WorkSpaces, see Provide Internet Access from Your WorkSpace. Note that WorkSpaces require an Internet connection to receive applications through Amazon WAM.

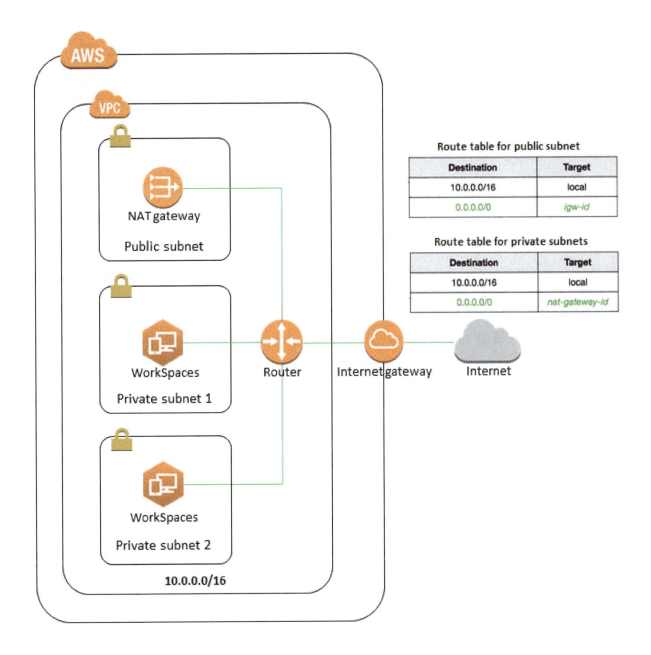

Route table for public subnet	
Destination	**Target**
10.0.0.0/16	local
0.0.0.0/0	igw-id

Route table for private subnets	
Destination	**Target**
10.0.0.0/16	local
0.0.0.0/0	nat-gateway-id

To configure your VPC for use with Amazon WorkSpaces, complete the following tasks. For more information about Amazon VPC, see the Amazon VPC User Guide.

Topics

- Step 1: Allocate an Elastic IP Address
- Step 2: Create a VPC
- Step 3: Add a Subnet
- Step 4: Verify the Route Tables

Step 1: Allocate an Elastic IP Address

Allocate an Elastic IP address for your NAT gateway as follows. Note that if you are using an alternative method of providing Internet access, you can skip this step.

To allocate an EIP

1. Open the Amazon VPC console at https://console.aws.amazon.com/vpc/.

2. In the navigation pane, choose **Elastic IPs**.

3. Choose **Allocate new address**.

4. On the **Allocate new address** page, choose **Allocate**.

Step 2: Create a VPC

Create a VPC with one public subnet and two private subnets as follows.

To set up a VPC

1. Open the Amazon VPC console at https://console.aws.amazon.com/vpc/.

2. On the VPC Dashboard, choose **Start VPC Wizard**.

3. Choose **VPC with Public and Private Subnets** and then choose **Select**.

4. Configure the VPC as follows:

    1. For **IPv4 CIDR block**, type the CIDR block for the VPC.

    2. For **VPC name**, type a name for the VPC.

5. Configure the public subnet as follows:

    1. For **IPv4 CIDR block**, type the CIDR block for the subnet.

    2. For **Availability Zone**, keep No Preference.

    3. For **Public subnet name**, type a name for the subnet.

6. Configure the first private subnet as follows:

    1. For **Private subnet's IPv4 CIDR**, type the CIDR block for the subnet.

    2. For **Availability Zone**, select the first one in the list (for example, us-west-2a).

    3. For **Private subnet name**, type a name for the subnet.

7. For **Elastic IP Allocation ID**, choose the Elastic IP address that you created. Note that if you are using an alternative method of providing Internet access, you can skip this step.

8. Choose **Create VPC**. Note that it takes several minutes to set up your VPC. After the VPC is created, choose **OK**.

Step 3: Add a Subnet

The VPC wizard created a VPC with one public subnet and one private subnet. Use the following procedure to add a second private subnet.

To add a subnet

1. In the navigation pane, choose **Subnets**.

2. Choose **Create Subnet**.

3. For **Name tag**, type a name for the subnet.

4. For **VPC**, select the VPC that you created.

5. For **Availability Zone**, select the second one in the list (for example, us-west-2b).

6. For **IPv4 CIDR block**, type the CIDR block for the subnet.

7. Choose **Yes, Create**.

Step 4: Verify the Route Tables

You can verify the route tables that the VPC Wizard created.

To verify the route tables

1. In the navigation pane, choose **Subnets**.

2. Select the public subnet.

3. On the **Route Table** tab, choose the ID of the route table (for example, rtb-12345678).

4. Select the route table. Type a name (for example, workspaces-public) and choose the save icon. On the **Routes** tab, verify that there is one route for local traffic and another route that sends all other traffic to the Internet gateway for the VPC.

5. Clear the search filter and select the other route table for the VPC, which is listed as the main route table for the VPC. Type a name (for example, workspaces-private) and choose the save icon. On the **Routes** tab, verify that there is one route for local traffic and another route that sends all other traffic to the NAT gateway.

Port Requirements for Amazon WorkSpaces

To connect to your WorkSpaces, the network that your Amazon WorkSpaces clients are connected to must have certain ports open to the IP address ranges for the various AWS services (grouped in subsets). These address ranges vary by AWS region. These same ports must also be open on any firewall running on the client. For more information about the AWS IP address ranges for different regions, see AWS IP Address Ranges in the *Amazon Web Services General Reference*.

Ports for Client Applications

The Amazon WorkSpaces client application requires outbound access on the following ports:

Port 443 (TCP)
This port is used for client application updates, registration, and authentication. The desktop client applications support the use of a proxy server for port 443 (HTTPS) traffic. To enable the use of a proxy server, open the client application, choose **Advanced Settings**, select **Use Proxy Server**, specify the address and port of the proxy server, and choose **Save**.
This port must be open to the following IP address ranges:

- The `AMAZON` subset in the `GLOBAL` region.
- The `AMAZON` subset in the region that the WorkSpace is in.
- The `AMAZON` subset in the `us-east-1` region.
- The `AMAZON` subset in the `us-west-2` region.
- The `S3` subset in the `us-west-2` region.

Port 4172 (UDP and TCP)
This port is used for streaming the WorkSpace desktop and health checks. It must be open to the PCoIP Gateway IP address ranges and health check servers in the region that the WorkSpace is in. For more information, see PCoIP Gateway and Health Check Servers.

Ports for Web Access

Amazon WorkSpaces Web Access requires inbound and outbound access for the following ports:

Port 53 (UDP)
This port is used to access DNS servers. It must be open to your DNS server IP addresses so that the client can resolve public domain names. This port requirement is optional if you are not using DNS servers for domain name resolution.

Port 80 (UDP and TCP)
This port is used for initial connections to `http://clients.amazonworkspaces.com`, which then switch to HTTPS. It must be open to all IP address ranges in the `EC2` subset in the region that the WorkSpace is in.

Port 443 (UDP and TCP)
This port is used for registration and authentication using HTTPS. It must be open to all IP address ranges in the `EC2` subset in the region that the WorkSpace is in.

Typically, the web browser randomly selects a source port in the high range to use for streaming traffic. Amazon WorkSpaces Web Access does not have control over the port the browser selects. You must ensure that return traffic to this port is allowed.

Amazon WorkSpaces Web Access prefers UDP over TCP for desktop streams, but falls back to TCP if UDP is not available as follows:

- Amazon WorkSpaces Web Access will work on Chrome even if all UDP ports are blocked except 53, 80, and 443, using TCP connections.

- Amazon WorkSpaces Web Access will not work on Firefox if all UDP ports are blocked except 53, 80, and 443. Additional UDP ports must be open to enable streaming.

Whitelisted Domains and Ports

For the Amazon WorkSpaces client application to be able to access the Amazon WorkSpaces service, the following domains and ports must be whitelisted on the network from which the client is trying to access the service.

Whitelisted domains and ports

Category	Whitelisted
Session Broker (PCM)	[See the AWS documentation website for more details]
PCoIP Session Gateway (PSG)	PCoIP Gateway and Health Check Servers
PCoIP Healthcheck (DRP)	[See the AWS documentation website for more details]
Device Metrics	https://device/-metrics/-us/-2/.amazon/.com/
Forrester Log Service	https://fls/-na/.amazon/.com/
Directory Settings	[See the AWS documentation website for more details] [See the AWS documentation website for more details] [See the AWS documentation website for more details] [See the AWS documentation website for more details]
CAPTCHA	https://opfcaptcha/-prod/.s3/.amazonaws/.com/
Client Auto-update	https://d2td7dqidlhjx7/.cloudfront/.net/
Registration Dependency	https://s3/.amazonaws/.com
Connectivity Check	https://connectivity/.amazonworkspaces/.com/
User Login Pages	https://.awsapps.com/ (where is the customer's domain)
Web client	[See the AWS documentation website for more details] [See the AWS documentation website for more details]
Web Access TURN Servers	[See the AWS documentation website for more details]

PCoIP Gateway and Health Check Servers

Amazon WorkSpaces uses PCoIP to stream the desktop session to clients over port 4172. Amazon WorkSpaces uses a small range of Amazon EC2 public IP addresses for its PCoIP gateway servers. This enables you to set more finely grained firewall policies for devices that access Amazon WorkSpaces.

Region	Public IP Address Range
US East (N. Virginia)	52.23.61.0 – 52.23.62.255
US West (Oregon)	54.244.46.0 – 54.244.47.255
Canada (Central)	35.183.255.0 - 35.183.255.255
EU (Ireland)	52.19.124.0 – 52.19.125.255
EU (Frankfurt)	52.59.127.0 - 52.59.127.255
EU (London)	35.176.32.0 - 35.176.32.255
Asia Pacific (Singapore)	52.76.127.0 – 52.76.127.255

Region	Public IP Address Range
Asia Pacific (Sydney)	54.153.254.0 – 54.153.254.255
Asia Pacific (Seoul)	13.124.247.0 - 13.124.247.255
Asia Pacific (Tokyo)	54.250.251.0 – 54.250.251.255
South America (São Paulo)	54.233.204.0 - 54.233.204.255

The Amazon WorkSpaces client application performs PCoIP health checks over port 4172. This validates whether TCP or UDP traffic streams from the Amazon WorkSpaces servers to the client applications. To do this successfully, your firewall policies must take into account the following regional PCoIP health check servers.

Region	Health check server
US East (N. Virginia)	drp-iad.amazonworkspaces.com
US West (Oregon)	drp-pdx.amazonworkspaces.com
Canada (Central)	drp-yul.amazonworkspaces.com
EU (Ireland)	drp-dub.amazonworkspaces.com
EU (Frankfurt)	drp-fra.amazonworkspaces.com
EU (London)	drp-lhr.amazonworkspaces.com
Asia Pacific (Singapore)	drp-sin.amazonworkspaces.com
Asia Pacific (Sydney)	drp-syd.amazonworkspaces.com
Asia Pacific (Seoul)	drp-icn.amazonworkspaces.com
Asia Pacific (Tokyo)	drp-nrt.amazonworkspaces.com
South America (São Paulo)	drp-gru.amazonworkspaces.com

Network Interfaces

Each WorkSpace has the following network interfaces:

- The primary network interface provides connectivity to the resources within your VPC as well as the Internet, and is used to join the WorkSpace to the directory.
- The management network interface is connected to a secure Amazon WorkSpaces management network. It is used for interactive streaming of the WorkSpace desktop to Amazon WorkSpaces clients, and to allow Amazon WorkSpaces to manage the WorkSpace.

Amazon WorkSpaces selects the IP address for the management network interface from various address ranges, depending on the region the WorkSpaces are created in. When a directory is registered, Amazon WorkSpaces tests the VPC CIDR and the route tables in your VPC to determine if these address ranges create a conflict. If a conflict is found in all available address ranges in the region, an error message is displayed and the directory is not registered. If you change the route tables in your VPC after the directory is registered, you might cause a conflict.

Do not modify or delete any of the network interfaces attached to a WorkSpace. Doing so might cause the WorkSpace to become unreachable.

Management Interface IP Ranges

The following table lists the IP address ranges used for the management network interface.

Region	IP Address Range
US East (N. Virginia)	172.31.0.0/16, 192.168.0.0/16, and 198.19.0.0/16
US West (Oregon)	172.31.0.0/16 and 192.168.0.0/16

Region	IP Address Range
Canada (Central)	198.19.0.0/16
EU (Ireland)	172.31.0.0/16 and 192.168.0.0/16
EU (Frankfurt)	198.19.0.0/16
EU (London)	198.19.0.0/16
Asia Pacific (Singapore)	198.19.0.0/16
Asia Pacific (Sydney)	172.31.0.0/16 and 192.168.0.0/16
Asia Pacific (Seoul)	198.19.0.0/16
Asia Pacific (Tokyo)	198.19.0.0/16
South America (São Paulo)	198.19.0.0/16

Management Interface Ports

When you create a WorkSpace, Amazon WorkSpaces opens the following ports to ensure that the WorkSpace is reachable and operates correctly. Do not install firewall software on your WorkSpace that blocks these ports.

- Inbound TCP on port 4172. This is used for establishment of the streaming connection.
- Inbound UDP on port 4172. This is used for streaming user input.
- Inbound TCP on port 8200. This is used for management and configuration of the WorkSpace.
- Outbound UDP on port 55002. This is used for PCoIP streaming. If your firewall uses stateful filtering, the ephemeral port 55002 is automatically opened to allow return communication. If your firewall uses stateless filtering, you need to open ephemeral ports 49152 - 65535 to allow return communication.

Primary Interface Ports

No matter which type of directory you have, the following ports must be open on the primary network interface of all WorkSpaces:

- For Internet connectivity, the following ports must be open outbound to all destinations and inbound from the WorkSpaces VPC. You need to add these manually to the security group for your WorkSpaces if you want them to have Internet access.

  - TCP 80 (HTTP)
  - TCP 443 (HTTPS)

- To communicate with the directory controllers, the following ports must be open between your WorkSpaces VPC and your directory controllers. For a Simple AD directory, the security group created by AWS Directory Service will have these ports configured correctly. For an AD Connector directory, you may need to adjust the default security group for the VPC to open these ports.

  - TCP/UDP 53 - DNS
  - TCP/UDP 88 - Kerberos authentication
  - UDP 123 - NTP
  - TCP 135 - RPC
  - UDP 137-138 - Netlogon
  - TCP 139 - Netlogon
  - TCP/UDP 389 - LDAP
  - TCP/UDP 445 - SMB
  - TCP 1024-65535 - Dynamic ports for RPC

  If any security or firewall software is installed on a WorkSpace that blocks any of these ports, the WorkSpace may not function correctly or may be unreachable.

- All WorkSpaces require that port 80 (HTTP) be open to IP address 169.254.169.254 to allow access to the EC2 metadata service. Any HTTP proxy assigned to your WorkSpaces must exclude 169.254.169.254.

Amazon WorkSpaces Client Network Requirements

Your Amazon WorkSpaces users access their WorkSpaces using the client application for a supported device or a web browser. To provide your users with a good experience with their WorkSpaces, verify that their client devices meet the following network requirements:

- The client device must have a broadband Internet connection.
- The network that the client device is connected to, and any firewall on the client device, must have certain ports open to the IP address ranges for various AWS services. For more information, see Port Requirements for Amazon WorkSpaces.
- The round trip time (RTT) from the client's network to the region that the WorkSpaces are in should be less than 100ms. If the RTT is between 100ms and 250ms, the user can access the WorkSpace but performance is degraded.
- If users will access their WorkSpaces through a virtual private network (VPN), the connection must support a maximum transmission unit (MTU) of at least 1200 bytes.
- The clients require HTTPS access to Amazon WorkSpaces resources hosted by the service and Amazon Simple Storage Service (Amazon S3). The client do not support proxy redirection at the application level. HTTPS access is required so that users can successfully complete registration and access their WorkSpaces.
- To allow access from PCoIP zero client devices, you must launch and configure an EC2 instance with PCoIP Connection Manager for Amazon WorkSpaces. For more information, see *Deploying the PCoIP Connection Manager for Amazon WorkSpaces* in the PCoIP Connection Manager User Guide.

You can verify that a client device meets the networking requirements as follows.

To verify client networking requirements

1. Open the Amazon WorkSpaces client. If this is the first time you have opened the client, you are prompted to type the registration code that you received in the invitation email.

2. Choose **Network** in the lower right corner of the client application. The client application tests the network connection, ports, and round trip time and reports the results of these tests.

3. Choose **Dismiss** to return to the sign in page.

Control Access to Amazon WorkSpaces Resources

By default, IAM users don't have permissions for Amazon WorkSpaces resources and operations. To allow IAM users to manage Amazon WorkSpaces resources, you must create an IAM policy that explicitly grants them permissions, and attach the policy to the IAM users or groups that require those permissions. For more information about IAM policies, see Permissions and Policies in the *IAM User Guide* guide.

Amazon WorkSpaces also creates an IAM role to allow the Amazon WorkSpaces service access to required resources.

For more information about IAM, see Identity and Access Management (IAM) and the IAM User Guide.

Example 1: Perform all Amazon WorkSpaces tasks The following policy statement grants an IAM user permission to perform all Amazon WorkSpaces tasks, including creating and managing directories, as well as running the quick setup procedure.

Note that although Amazon WorkSpaces fully supports the `Action` and `Resource` elements when using the API and command-line tools, you must set them both to "*" in order to use the Amazon WorkSpaces console successfully.

```
1  {
2    "Version": "2012-10-17",
3    "Statement": [
4      {
5        "Effect": "Allow",
6        "Action": [
7          "workspaces:*",
8          "ds:*",
9          "iam:PassRole",
10         "iam:GetRole",
11         "iam:CreateRole",
12         "iam:PutRolePolicy",
13         "kms:ListAliases",
14         "kms:ListKeys",
15         "ec2:CreateVpc",
16         "ec2:CreateSubnet",
17         "ec2:CreateNetworkInterface",
18         "ec2:CreateInternetGateway",
19         "ec2:CreateRouteTable",
20         "ec2:CreateRoute",
21         "ec2:CreateTags",
22         "ec2:CreateSecurityGroup",
23         "ec2:DescribeInternetGateways",
24         "ec2:DescribeRouteTables",
25         "ec2:DescribeVpcs",
26         "ec2:DescribeSubnets",
27         "ec2:DescribeNetworkInterfaces",
28         "ec2:DescribeAvailabilityZones",
29         "ec2:AttachInternetGateway",
30         "ec2:AssociateRouteTable",
31         "ec2:AuthorizeSecurityGroupEgress",
32         "ec2:AuthorizeSecurityGroupIngress",
33         "ec2:DeleteSecurityGroup",
34         "ec2:DeleteNetworkInterface",
35         "ec2:RevokeSecurityGroupEgress",
36         "ec2:RevokeSecurityGroupIngress",
37         "workdocs:RegisterDirectory",
```

```
38        "workdocs:DeregisterDirectory",
39        "workdocs:AddUserToGroup",
40        "workdocs:RemoveUserFromGroup"
41      ],
42      "Resource": "*"
43    }
44  ]
45 }
```

Example 2: Perform WorkSpace-specific tasks The following policy statement grants an IAM user permission to perform WorkSpace-specific tasks, such as launching and removing WorkSpaces. The user can perform some tasks on the WorkSpaces directory, such as enabling or disabling the settings for Internet access, local administrator access, and maintenance mode.

```
1 {
2   "Version": "2012-10-17",
3   "Statement": [
4     {
5       "Effect": "Allow",
6       "Action": [
7         "workspaces:*",
8         "ds:*"
9       ],
10      "Resource": "*"
11    }
12  ]
13 }
```

To also grant the user the ability to enable Amazon WorkDocs for users within Amazon WorkSpaces, add the `workdocs` operations shown here:

```
1 {
2   "Version": "2012-10-17",
3   "Statement": [
4     {
5       "Effect": "Allow",
6       "Action": [
7         "workspaces:*",
8         "ds:*",
9         "workdocs:AddUserToGroup",
10        "workdocs:RemoveUserFromGroup"
11      ],
12      "Resource": "*"
13    }
14  ]
15 }
```

To also grant the user the ability to use the Launch WorkSpaces wizard, add the `kms` operations shown here:

```
1 {
2   "Version": "2012-10-17",
3   "Statement": [
4     {
5       "Effect": "Allow",
6       "Action": [
7         "workspaces:*",
```

```
 8        "ds:*",
 9        "workdocs:AddUserToGroup",
10        "workdocs:RemoveUserFromGroup",
11        "kms:ListAliases",
12        "kms:ListKeys"
13      ],
14      "Resource": "*"
15    }
16  ]
17 }
```

To grant the user the ability to perform WorkSpaces-specific tasks except for certificate tasks, add a statement to deny the certificate operations:

```
 1 {
 2   "Version": "2012-10-17",
 3   "Statement": [
 4     {
 5       "Effect": "Allow",
 6       "Action": [
 7         "workspaces:*",
 8         "ds:*"
 9       ],
10       "Resource": "*"
11     },
12     {
13       "Effect": "Deny",
14       "Action": [
15         "workspaces:DeleteCertificate",
16         "workspaces:ImportCertificate",
17         "workspaces:DescribeCertificates"
18       ],
19       "Resource": "*"
20     }
21   ]
22 }
```

Specifying Amazon WorkSpaces Resources in an IAM Policy

To specify an Amazon WorkSpaces resource in the `Resource` element of the policy statement, you need to use the Amazon Resource Name (ARN) of the resource. You control access to your Amazon WorkSpaces resources by either allowing or denying permissions to use the API actions specified in the `Action` element of your IAM policy statement. Amazon WorkSpaces defines ARNs for WorkSpaces and bundles.

WorkSpace ARN

A WorkSpace ARN has the following syntax:

```
1 arn:aws:workspaces:region:account_id:workspace/workspace_identifier
```

region
The region that the WorkSpace is in (for example, `us-east-2`).

account_id
The ID of the AWS account, with no hyphens (for example, `123456789012`).

workspace_identifier
The ID of the WorkSpace (for example, `ws-0123456789`).

The following is the format of the `Resource` element of a policy statement that identifies a specific WorkSpace:

```
1  "Resource": "arn:aws:workspaces:region:account_id:workspace/workspace_identifier"
```

You can use the * wildcard to specify all WorkSpaces that belong to a specific account in a specific region.

Bundle ARN

A bundle ARN has the following syntax:

```
1  arn:aws:workspaces:region:account_id:workspacebundle/bundle_identifier
```

region
The region that the WorkSpace is in (for example, `us-east-2`).

account_id
The ID of the AWS account, with no hyphens (for example, `123456789012`).

bundle_identifier
The ID of the WorkSpace bundle (for example, `wsb-0123456789`).

The following is the format of the `Resource` element of a policy statement that identifies a specific bundle:

```
1  "Resource": "arn:aws:workspaces:region:account_id:workspacebundle/bundle_identifier"
```

You can use the * wildcard to specify all bundles that belong to a specific account in a specific region.

API Actions with No Support for Resource-Level Permissions

You can't specify a resource ARN with the following API actions:

- `CreateTags`
- `DeleteTags`
- `DescribeTags`
- `DescribeWorkspaceDirectories`
- `DescribeWorkspaces`
- `DescribeWorkspacesConnectionStatus`

For API actions that don't support resource-level permissions, you must specify the following resource statement:

```
1  "Resource": "*"
```

Restrict WorkSpaces Access to Trusted Devices

By default, users can access their WorkSpaces from any supported device that is connected to the Internet. If your company limits corporate data access to trusted devices (also known as managed devices), you can restrict WorkSpaces access to trusted devices with valid certificates.

When you enable this feature, Amazon WorkSpaces uses certificate-based authentication to determine whether a device is trusted. If the WorkSpaces client application can't verify that a device is trusted, it blocks attempts to log in or reconnect from the device.

For each directory, you can import up to two root certificates. If you import two root certificates, Amazon WorkSpaces presents them both to the client and the client finds the first valid matching certificate that chains up to either of the root certificates.

Important
This feature is supported for Windows computers and Mac computers.

Step 1: Create the Certificates

This feature requires two types of certificates: root certificates generated by an internal Certificate Authority (CA) and client certificates that chain up to a root certificate.

Requirements

- Certificates must be Base64-encoded certificate files in CRT, CERT, or PEM format.
- Certificates must include a Common Name.
- The maximum length of certificate chain supported is 4.
- Amazon WorkSpaces does not currently support device revocation mechanisms, such as certificate revocation lists (CRL) or Online Certificate Status Protocol (OCSP), for client certificates.
- Use a strong encryption algorithm. We recommend SHA256 with RSA, SHA256 with ECDSA, SHA381 with ECDSA, or SHA512 with ECDSA.
- For macOS, if the device certificate is in the system keychain, we recommend that you authorize the WorkSpaces client application to access those certificates. Otherwise, users must enter keychain credentials when they log in or reconnect.

Step 2: Deploy Client Certificates to the Trusted Devices

You must install client certificates on the trusted devices for your users. You can use your preferred solution to install certificates to your fleet of client devices; for example, System Center Configuration Manager (SCCM) or mobile device management (MDM). Note that SCCM and MDM can optionally perform a security posture assessment to determine whether the devices meet your corporate policies to access WorkSpaces.

On Windows, the WorkSpaces client application searches for client certificates in both the user and root certificate stores. On macOS, the WorkSpaces client application searches for client certificates in the entire keychain.

Step 3: Configure the Restriction

After you have deployed the client certificates on the trusted devices, you can enable restricted access at the directory level. This requires the WorkSpaces client application to validate the certificate on a device before allowing a user to log in to a WorkSpace.

To configure the restriction

1. Open the Amazon WorkSpaces console at https://console.aws.amazon.com/workspaces/.

2. In the navigation pane, choose **Directories**.

3. Select the directory and then choose **Actions, Update Details**.

4. Expand **Access Control Options**.

5. [Windows] Choose **Only Allow Trusted Windows Devices to Access WorkSpaces**.

6. [macOS] Choose **Only Allow Trusted macOS Devices to Access WorkSpaces**.

7. Import up to two root certificates. For each root certificate, do the following:

    1. Choose **Import**.

    2. Copy the body of the certificate to the form.

    3. Choose **Import**.

8. Choose **Update and Exit**.

Provide Internet Access from Your WorkSpace

We recommend that you launch your WorkSpaces in private subnets in your virtual private cloud (VPC) and use one of the following options to allow your WorkSpaces to access the Internet:

Options

- Configure a NAT gateway in your VPC. For more information, see Configure a VPC for Amazon WorkSpaces.
- Configure automatic assignment of public IP addresses. For more information, see Configure Automatic IP Addresses.
- Manually assign public IP addresses to your WorkSpaces. For more information, see Manually Assign IP Addresses.

With any of these options, you must ensure that the security group for your WorkSpaces allows outbound traffic on ports 80 (HTTP) and 443 (HTTPS) to all destinations (0.0.0.0/0).

Amazon WAM

If you are using Amazon WorkSpaces Application Manager (Amazon WAM) to deploy applications to your WorkSpaces, your WorkSpaces must have access to the Internet.

Manually Assign IP Addresses

You can manually assign an Elastic IP address to a WorkSpace.

Prerequisites

- Your VPC must have an attached Internet gateway. For more information, see Attaching an Internet Gateway in the *Amazon VPC User Guide.*
- The route table for the WorkSpaces subnets must have one route for local traffic and another route that sends all other traffic to the Internet gateway.

To assign an Elastic IP address to a WorkSpace

1. Open the Amazon WorkSpaces console at https://console.aws.amazon.com/workspaces/.

2. In the navigation pane, choose **WorkSpaces**.

3. Expand the row for the WorkSpace and note the value of **WorkSpace IP**. This is the primary private IP address of WorkSpace.

4. Open the Amazon EC2 console at https://console.aws.amazon.com/ec2/.

5. In the navigation pane, choose **Elastic IPs**. If you do not have an available Elastic IP address, choose **Allocate new address** and follow the directions.

6. In the navigation pane, choose **Network Interfaces**.

7. Select the network interface for your WorkSpace. Note that the value of **VPC ID** matches the ID of your WorkSpaces VPC and the value of **Primary private IPv4 IP** matches the primary private IP address of the WorkSpace that you noted earlier.

8. Choose **Actions, Associate Address**.

9. On the **Associate Elastic IP Address** page, choose an Elastic IP address from **Address** and then choose **Associate Address**.

Security Groups for Your WorkSpaces

When you register a directory with Amazon WorkSpaces, it creates two security groups, one for directory controllers and another for WorkSpaces in the directory. The security group for directory controllers has a name that consists of the directory identifier followed by _controllers (for example, d-92673056e8_controllers) and the security group for WorkSpaces has a name that consists of the directory identifier followed by _workspacesMembers (for example, d-926720fc18_workspacesMembers).

You have the option to have an additional security group for WorkSpaces. After you add the security group to the directory, it is associated with new WorkSpaces that you launch or existing WorkSpaces that you rebuild.

To add a security group to a directory

1. Open the Amazon WorkSpaces console at https://console.aws.amazon.com/workspaces/.

2. In the navigation pane, choose **Directories**.

3. Select the directory and choose **Actions, Update Details**.

4. Expand **Security Group** and select a security group.

5. Choose **Update and Exit**.

IP Access Control Groups for Your WorkSpaces

An *IP access control group* acts as a virtual firewall that controls the IP addresses from which users are allowed to access their WorkSpaces. You can associate each IP access control group with one or more directories. You can associate up to 25 IP access control groups with each directory.

There is a default IP access control group associated with each directory. The default group allows all traffic. If you associate an IP access control group with a directory, the default IP access control group is disassociated.

To specify the IP addresses and ranges of IP addresses for your trusted networks, add rules to your IP access control groups. If your users access their WorkSpaces through a NAT gateway or VPN, you must create rules that allow traffic from the IP addresses for the NAT gateway or VPN.

Create an IP Access Control Group

You can create up to 25 IP access control groups. Each IP access control group can contain up to 10 rules.

To create an IP access control group

1. Open the Amazon WorkSpaces console at https://console.aws.amazon.com/workspaces/.
2. In the navigation pane, choose **IP Access Controls**.
3. Choose **Create IP Group**.
4. In the **Create IP Group** dialog box, type a name and description for the group and choose **Create**.
5. Select the group and choose **Edit**.
6. For each IP address, choose **Add Rule**. For **Source**, type the IP address or IP address range. For **Description**, type a description. When you are done adding rules, choose **Save**.

Associate an IP Access Control Group with a Directory

You can associate an IP access control group with a directory to ensure that WorkSpaces are accessed only from trusted networks.

If you associate an IP access control group that has no rules with a directory, this blocks all access to all WorkSpaces.

To associate an IP access control group with a directory

1. Open the Amazon WorkSpaces console at https://console.aws.amazon.com/workspaces/.
2. In the navigation pane, choose **Directories**.
3. Select the directory and choose **Actions**, **Update Details**.
4. Expand **IP Access Control Groups** and select one or more IP access control groups.
5. Choose **Update and Exit**.

Copy an IP Access Control Group

You can use an existing IP access control group as a base for creating a new IP access control group.

To create an IP access control group from an existing one

1. Open the Amazon WorkSpaces console at https://console.aws.amazon.com/workspaces/.
2. In the navigation pane, choose **IP Access Controls**.

3. Select the group and choose **Actions, Copy to New**.

4. In the **Copy IP Group** dialog box, type a name and description for the new group and choose **Copy Group**.

5. (Optional) To modify the rules copied from the original group, select the new group and choose **Edit**. Add, update, or remove rules as needed. Choose **Save**.

Delete an IP Access Control Group

You can delete a rule from an IP access control group at any time. If you remove a rule that was used to allow a connection to a WorkSpace, the user is disconnected from the WorkSpace.

Before you can delete an IP access control group, you must disassociate it from any directories.

To delete an IP access control group

1. Open the Amazon WorkSpaces console at https://console.aws.amazon.com/workspaces/.

2. In the navigation pane, choose **Directories**.

3. For each directory that is associated with the IP access control group, select the directory and choose **Actions, Update Details**. Expand **IP Access Control Groups**, clear the checkbox for the IP access control group, and choose **Update and Exit**.

4. In the navigation pane, choose **IP Access Controls**.

5. Select the group and choose **Actions, Delete IP Group**.

Set Up PCoIP Zero Client for WorkSpaces

If your zero client device has firmware version 6.0.0 or later, your users can connect to their WorkSpaces directly. Otherwise, if the firmware is between 4.6.0 and 6.0.0, you must set up Teradici PCoIP Connection Manager for Amazon WorkSpaces and provide your users with server URIs to connect to their WorkSpaces through Teradici PCoIP Connection Manager for Amazon WorkSpaces.

To set up PCoIP Connection Manager for Amazon WorkSpaces on an EC2 instance, go to AWS Marketplace and find an Amazon Machine Image (AMI) that you can use to launch an instance with PCoIP Connection Manager. For more information, see *Deploying the PCoIP Connection Manager for Amazon WorkSpaces* in the PCoIP Connection Manager User Guide.

For information about setting up and connecting with a PCoIP zero client device, see PCoIP Zero Client in the *Amazon WorkSpaces User Guide*.

Manage Directories for Amazon WorkSpaces

Amazon WorkSpaces uses a directory to store and manage information for your WorkSpaces and users. You can use one of the following options:

- AD Connector — Use your existing on-premises Microsoft Active Directory. Users can sign into their WorkSpaces using their on-premises credentials and access on-premises resources from their WorkSpaces.
- Microsoft AD — Create a Microsoft Active Directory hosted on AWS.
- Simple AD — Create a directory that is compatible with Microsoft Active Directory, powered by Samba 4, and hosted on AWS.
- Cross trust — Create a trust relationship between your Microsoft AD directory and your on-premises domain.

For tutorials that demonstrate how to set up these directories and launch WorkSpaces, see Launch a Virtual Desktop Using Amazon WorkSpaces.

After you create a directory, you'll perform most directory administration tasks using tools such as the Active Directory Administration Tools. You can perform some directory administration tasks using the Amazon WorkSpaces console and other tasks using Group Policy.

Topics

- Register a Directory with Amazon WorkSpaces
- Update Directory Details for Your WorkSpaces
- Delete the Directory for Your WorkSpaces
- Set Up Active Directory Administration Tools for Amazon WorkSpaces
- Manage Your WorkSpaces Using Group Policy

Register a Directory with Amazon WorkSpaces

To allow Amazon WorkSpaces to use an existing AWS Directory Service directory, you must register it with Amazon WorkSpaces. After you register a directory, you can launch WorkSpaces in the directory.

To register a directory

1. Open the Amazon WorkSpaces console at https://console.aws.amazon.com/workspaces/.

2. In the navigation pane, choose **Directories**.

3. Select the directory.

4. Choose **Actions, Register**.

5. For **Enable Amazon WorkDocs**, choose **Yes** to register the directory for use with Amazon WorkDocs or **No** otherwise. **Note**
This option is only displayed if Amazon WorkDocs is available in the region.

6. Choose **Register**. Initially the value of **Registered** is REGISTERING. After registration is complete, the value is Yes.

When you are finished using the directory with Amazon WorkSpaces, you can deregister it. Note that you must deregister a directory before you can delete it. If you have any Amazon WAM applications assigned to your users, you must remove those assignments before you can delete a directory. For more information, see Removing Application Assignments in the *Amazon WAM Administration Guide*.

To deregister a directory

1. Open the Amazon WorkSpaces console at https://console.aws.amazon.com/workspaces/.

2. In the navigation pane, choose **Directories**.

3. Select the directory.

4. Choose **Actions, Deregister**.

5. When prompted for confirmation, choose **Deregister**. After deregistration is complete, the value of **Registered** is No.

Update Directory Details for Your WorkSpaces

You can complete the following directory management tasks using the Amazon WorkSpaces console.

Topics

- Select an Organizational Unit
- Configure Automatic IP Addresses
- Control Device Access
- Manage Local Administrator Permissions
- Update the AD Connector Account (AD Connector)
- Multi-factor Authentication (AD Connector)

Select an Organizational Unit

WorkSpace machine accounts are placed in the default organizational unit (OU) for the WorkSpaces directory. Initially, the machine accounts are placed in the Computers OU of your directory or the directory that your AD Connector is connected to. You can select a different OU from your directory or connected directory, or specify an OU in a separate target domain. Note that you can select only one OU per directory.

After you select a new OU, the machine accounts for all WorkSpaces that are created or rebuilt are placed in the newly selected OU.

To select an organizational unit

1. Open the Amazon WorkSpaces console at https://console.aws.amazon.com/workspaces/.

2. In the navigation pane, choose **Directories**.

3. Select your directory and then choose **Actions, Update Details**.

4. Expand **Target Domain and Organizational Unit**.

5. To find an OU, you can type all or part of the OU name and choose **Search OU**. Alternatively, you can choose **List all OU** to list all OUs.

6. Select the OU and choose **Update and Exit**.

7. (Optional) Rebuild the existing WorkSpaces to update the OU. For more information, see Rebuild a WorkSpace.

To specify a target domain and organizational unit

1. Open the Amazon WorkSpaces console at https://console.aws.amazon.com/workspaces/.

2. In the navigation pane, choose **Directories**.

3. Select your directory and then choose **Actions, Update Details**.

4. Expand **Target Domain and Organizational Unit**.

5. For **Selected OU**, type the full LDAP distinguished name for the target domain and OU and then choose **Update and Exit**. For example, **OU=WorkSpaces_machines,DC=machines,DC=example,DC=com**.

6. (Optional) Rebuild the existing WorkSpaces to update the OU. For more information, see Rebuild a WorkSpace.

Configure Automatic IP Addresses

After you enable automatic assignment of public IP addresses, each WorkSpace that you launch is assigned a public IP address. This allows the WorkSpaces to access the Internet. WorkSpaces that exist at the time you enable automatic assignment do not receive a public IP address until you rebuild them.

Note that you do not need to enable automatic assignment of public IP access if you configured your VPC with a NAT gateway. For more information, see Configure a VPC for Amazon WorkSpaces.

Prerequisites

- Your VPC must have an attached Internet gateway. For more information, see Attaching an Internet Gateway in the *Amazon VPC User Guide*.
- The route table for the WorkSpaces subnets must have one route for local traffic and another route that sends all other traffic to the Internet gateway.

To configure public IP addresses

1. Open the Amazon WorkSpaces console at https://console.aws.amazon.com/workspaces/.

2. In the navigation pane, choose **Directories**.

3. Select the directory for your WorkSpaces.

4. Choose **Actions**, **Update Details**.

5. Expand **Access to Internet** and select **Enable** or **Disable**.

6. Choose **Update**.

Control Device Access

You can specify the types of devices that have access to WorkSpaces. In addition, you restrict access to WorkSpaces to trusted devices (also known as managed devices).

To control device access to WorkSpaces

1. Open the Amazon WorkSpaces console at https://console.aws.amazon.com/workspaces/.

2. In the navigation pane, choose **Directories**.

3. Select the directory and then choose **Actions**, **Update Details**.

4. Expand **Access Control Options** and find the **Other Platforms** section. By default, WorkSpaces Web Access is disabled and users can access their WorkSpaces from their iOS devices, Android devices, Chromebooks, and PCoIP zero client devices.

5. Select the device types to enable and clear the device types to disable. To block access from all selected device types, choose **Block**.

6. (Optional) You can restrict access to trusted devices. For more information, see Restrict WorkSpaces Access to Trusted Devices.

7. Choose **Update and Exit**.

Manage Local Administrator Permissions

You can specify whether users are local administrators on their WorkSpaces, which enables them to install application and modify settings on their WorkSpaces. Users are local administrators by default. If you modify this setting, the change applies to all new WorkSpaces that you create and any WorkSpaces that you rebuild.

To modify local administrator permissions

1. Open the Amazon WorkSpaces console at https://console.aws.amazon.com/workspaces/.

2. In the navigation pane, choose **Directories**.

3. Select your directory and then choose **Actions**, **Update Details**.

4. Expand **Local Administrator Setting**.

5. To ensure that users are local administrators, choose **Enable**. Otherwise, choose **Disable**.

6. Choose **Update and Exit**.

Update the AD Connector Account (AD Connector)

You can update the AD Connector account that is used to read users and groups and join Amazon WorkSpaces machine accounts to your AD Connector directory.

To update the AD Connector account

1. Open the Amazon WorkSpaces console at https://console.aws.amazon.com/workspaces/.

2. In the navigation pane, choose **Directories**.

3. Select your directory and then choose **Actions**, **Update Details**.

4. Expand **Update AD Connector Account**.

5. Type the username and password for the new account.

6. Choose **Update and Exit**.

Multi-factor Authentication (AD Connector)

You can enable multi-factor authentication for your AD Connector directory.

To enable multi-factor authentication

1. Open the Amazon WorkSpaces console at https://console.aws.amazon.com/workspaces/.

2. In the navigation pane, choose **Directories**.

3. Select your directory and then choose **Actions**, **Update Details**.

4. Expand **Multi-Factor Authentication** and then select **Enable Multi-Factor Authentication**.

5. For **RADIUS server IP address(es)**, type the IP addresses of your RADIUS server endpoints separated by commas, or type the IP address of your RADIUS server load balancer.

6. For **Port**, type the port that your RADIUS server is using for communications. Your on-premises network must allow inbound traffic over the default RADIUS server port (1812) from AD Connector.

7. For **Shared secret code** and **Confirm shared secret code**, type the shared secret code for your RADIUS server.

8. For **Protocol**, choose the protocol for your RADIUS server.

9. For **Server timeout**, type the time, in seconds, to wait for the RADIUS server to respond. This value must be between 1 and 20.

10. For **Max retries**, type the number of times to attempt communication with the RADIUS server. This value must be between 0 and 10.

11. Choose **Update and Exit**.

Multi-factor authentication is available when **RADIUS status** is **Enabled**. While multi-factor authentication is being set up, users cannot log in to their WorkSpaces.

Delete the Directory for Your WorkSpaces

You can delete the directory for your WorkSpaces if it is no longer in use by other WorkSpaces or applications such as Amazon WorkDocs, Amazon WorkMail, or Amazon Chime. Note that you must deregister a directory before you can delete it.

To delete a directory

1. Open the Amazon WorkSpaces console at https://console.aws.amazon.com/workspaces/.

2. In the navigation pane, choose **Directories**.

3. Select the directory and choose **Actions**, **Deregister**.

4. When prompted for confirmation, choose **Deregister**.

5. Select the directory again and choose **Actions**, **Delete**.

6. When prompted for confirmation, choose **Delete**.

Set Up Active Directory Administration Tools for Amazon WorkSpaces

You'll perform most administrative tasks for your WorkSpaces directory using directory management tools, such as the Active Directory Administration Tools. However, you'll use Amazon WorkSpaces console to perform some directory-related tasks. For more information, see Manage Directories for Amazon WorkSpaces.

If you create a Microsoft AD or Simple AD with five or more WorkSpaces, we recommend that you centralize administration on an Amazon EC2 instance. Although it is possible to install the directory management tools on a WorkSpace, there are limitations, and using an instance is a more robust solution.

To set up the Active Directory Administration Tools

1. Launch a Windows instance and join it to your WorkSpaces directory.

   You can join an Amazon EC2 Windows instance to your directory domain when you launch the instance. For more information, see Joining a Windows Instance to an AWS Directory Service Domain in the *Amazon EC2 User Guide for Windows Instances*.

   Alternatively, you can join the instance to your directory manually. For more information, see Manually Add a Windows Instance (Simple AD and Microsoft AD) in the *AWS Directory Service Administration Guide*.

2. Install the Active Directory Administration Tools on the instance. For more information, see Installing the Active Directory Administration Tools in the *AWS Directory Service Administration Guide*.

3. Run the tools as a directory administrator as follows:

   1. Open the **Administrative Tools**.

   2. Hold down the Shift key, right-click the tool shortcut, and choose **Run as different user**.

   3. Type the username and password for the administrator. With Simple AD, the username is **Administrator** and with Microsoft AD, the administrator is **Admin**.

You can now perform directory administration tasks using the Active Directory tools that you are familiar with. For example, you can use the Active Directory Users and Computers Tool to add users, remove users, promote a user to directory administrator, or reset a user password. Note that you must be logged into your Windows instance as a user that has permissions to manage users in the directory.

To promote a user to a directory administrator

1. Open the Active Directory Users and Computers tool.

2. Navigate to the **Users** folder under your domain and select the user to promote.

3. Choose **Action, Properties**.

4. In the user properties dialog box, choose **Member of**.

5. Add the user to the following groups and choose **OK**.

   - Administrators
   - Domain Admins
   - Enterprise Admins
   - Group Policy Creator Owners
   - Schema Admins

To add or remove users
You can use whichever Active Directory tools you are familiar with to manage user objects. Note that before you can remove a user, you must delete the WorkSpace assigned to that user. For more information, see Delete a WorkSpace.

To reset a user password
When you reset the password for an existing user, do not set **User must change password at next logon**. Otherwise, the users cannot connect to their WorkSpaces. Instead, assign a secure temporary password to each user and then ask the users to manually change their passwords from within the WorkSpace the next time they log on.

Manage Your WorkSpaces Using Group Policy

You can apply Group Policy settings to the WorkSpaces or users that are part of your WorkSpaces directory.

We recommend that you create an organizational unit for your WorkSpaces machine accounts and an organizational unit for your WorkSpaces user accounts.

Group Policy settings can affect a WorkSpace user's experience as follows:

- Depending on the number of custom Group Policy settings applied to a WorkSpace, a user's first login to their WorkSpace after it is launched or rebooted can take several minutes.
- Changes to Group Policy settings can cause an active session to be closed when a user is not connected to the WorkSpace.
- Some Group Policy settings force a user to log off when they are disconnected from a session. Any applications that a user has open on the WorkSpace are closed.
- Implementing an interactive logon message to display a logon banner prevents users from being able to access their WorkSpace. The interactive logon message Group Policy setting is not currently supported by Amazon WorkSpaces.

Topics

- Install the Group Policy Administrative Template
- Local Printer Support
- Clipboard Redirection
- Setting the Session Resume Timeout

Install the Group Policy Administrative Template

To use the Group Policy settings that are specific to Amazon WorkSpaces, you need to install the Group Policy administrative template. Perform the following procedure on a directory administration WorkSpace or Amazon EC2 instance that is joined to your directory.

To install the Group Policy administrative template

1. From a running WorkSpace, make a copy of the `pcoip.adm` file in the `C:\Program Files (x86)\Teradici \PCoIP Agent\configuration` directory.

2. Open the Group Policy Management tool and navigate to the organizational unit in your domain that contains your WorkSpaces machine accounts.

3. Open the context (right-click) menu for the machine account organizational unit and choose **Create a GPO in this domain, and link it here**.

4. In the **New GPO** dialog box, enter a descriptive name for the Group Policy object, such as **WorkSpaces Machine Policies**, and leave **Source Starter GPO** set to **(none)**. Choose **OK**.

5. Open the context (right-click) menu for the new Group Policy object and choose **Edit**.

6. In the Group Policy Management Editor, choose **Computer Configuration**, **Policies**, and **Administrative Templates**. Choose **Action**, **Add/Remove Templates** from the main menu.

7. In the **Add/Remove Templates** dialog box, choose **Add**, select the `pcoip.adm` file copied previously, and then choose **Open**, **Close**.

8. Close the Group Policy Management Editor. You can now use this Group Policy object to modify the Group Policy settings that are specific to Amazon WorkSpaces.

Local Printer Support

By default, Amazon WorkSpaces disables local printer redirection. You can use Group Policy settings to enable this feature if needed.

The Group Policy setting change takes effect after the WorkSpace's next Group Policy settings update and the session is restarted.

To enable or disable local printer support

1. Make sure that the most recent Amazon WorkSpaces Group Policy administrative template is installed in your domain.

2. Open the Group Policy Management tool and navigate to and select the WorkSpaces Group Policy object for your WorkSpaces machine accounts. Choose **Action**, **Edit** in the main menu.

3. In the Group Policy Management Editor, choose **Computer Configuration**, **Policies**, **Administrative Templates**, **Classic Administrative Templates**, **PCoIP Session Variables**, and **Overridable Administration Defaults**.

4. Open the **Configure remote printing** setting.

5. In the **Configure remote printing** dialog box, choose **Enabled** or **Disabled**, and then choose **OK**.

By default, local printer auto-redirection is disabled. You can use Group Policy settings to enable this feature so that your local printer is set as the default printer every time you connect to your WorkSpace.

To enable or disable local printer auto-redirection

1. Make sure that the most recent Amazon WorkSpaces Group Policy administrative template is installed in your domain.

2. Open the Group Policy Management tool and navigate to and select the WorkSpaces Group Policy object for your WorkSpaces machine accounts. Choose **Action**, **Edit** in the main menu.

3. In the Group Policy Management Editor, choose **Computer Configuration**, **Policies**, **Administrative Templates**, **Classic Administrative Templates**, **PCoIP Session Variables**, and **Overridable Administration Defaults**.

4. Open the **Configure remote printing** setting.

5. In the **Configure remote printing** dialog box, choose **Enabled**, set or clear **Automatically set default printer**, and then choose **OK**.

Clipboard Redirection

By default, Amazon WorkSpaces supports clipboard redirection. You can use Group Policy settings to disable this feature if needed.

The Group Policy setting change takes effect after the WorkSpace's next Group Policy settings update and the session is restarted.

To enable or disable clipboard redirection

1. Make sure that the most recent Amazon WorkSpaces Group Policy administrative template is installed in your domain.

2. Open the Group Policy Management tool and navigate to and select the WorkSpaces Group Policy object for your WorkSpaces machine accounts. Choose **Action**, **Edit** in the main menu.

3. In the Group Policy Management Editor, choose **Computer Configuration**, **Policies**, **Administrative Templates**,**Classic Administrative Templates**, **PCoIP Session Variables**, and **Overridable Administration Defaults**.

4. Open the **Configure clipboard redirection** setting.

5. In the **Configure clipboard redirection** dialog box, choose **Enabled** and set the **Configure clipboard redirection** option to the desired setting, enabled or disabled, and choose **OK**.

Known Limitation

With clipboard redirection enabled on the WorkSpace, if you copy content that is larger than 890KB from a Microsoft Office application, the application might become slow or unresponsive for up to 5 seconds.

Setting the Session Resume Timeout

When using the Amazon WorkSpaces client applications, an interruption of network connectivity causes an active session to be disconnected. This can be caused by events such as closing the laptop lid, or the loss of your wireless network connection. The Amazon WorkSpaces client applications for Windows and OS X attempt to reconnect the session automatically if network connectivity is regained within a certain amount of time. The default session resume timeout is 20 minutes, but you can modify that value for WorkSpaces that are controlled by your domain's Group Policy settings.

The Group Policy setting change takes effect after the WorkSpace's next Group Policy settings update and the session is restarted.

To set the automatic session resume timeout value

1. Make sure that the most recent Amazon WorkSpaces Group Policy administrative template is installed in your domain.

2. Open the Group Policy Management tool and navigate to and select the WorkSpaces Group Policy object for your WorkSpaces machine accounts. Choose **Action**, **Edit** in the main menu.

3. In the Group Policy Management Editor, choose **Computer Configuration, Policies, Administrative Templates, Classic Administrative Templates**, and **PCoIP Session Variables**.

   To allow the user to override your setting, choose **Overridable Administration Defaults**; otherwise, choose **Not Overridable Administration Defaults**.

4. Open the **Configure Session Automatic Reconnection Policy** setting.

5. In the **Configure Session Automatic Reconnection Policy** dialog box, choose **Enabled**, set the **Configure Session Automatic Reconnection Policy** option to the desired timeout, in minutes, and choose **OK**.

Launch a Virtual Desktop Using Amazon WorkSpaces

With Amazon WorkSpaces, you can provision virtual, cloud-based Microsoft Windows desktops for your users, known as *WorkSpaces*.

Amazon WorkSpaces uses a directory to store and manage information for your WorkSpaces and users. You can create a Simple AD directory or a Microsoft AD directory, connect to an existing Microsoft Active Directory using Active Directory Connector, or create a trust relationship between your Microsoft AD directory and your on-premises domain.

The following tutorials show you how launch a WorkSpace using the supported directory service options.

Topics

- Launch a WorkSpace Using Microsoft AD
- Launch a WorkSpace Using Simple AD
- Launch a WorkSpace Using AD Connector
- Launch a WorkSpace Using a Trusted Domain

Launch a WorkSpace Using Microsoft AD

Amazon WorkSpaces enables you to provision virtual, cloud-based Microsoft Windows desktops for your users, known as *WorkSpaces*.

Amazon WorkSpaces uses directories to store and manage information for your WorkSpaces and users. For your directory, you can choose from Simple AD, AD Connector, or AWS Directory Service for Microsoft Active Directory (Enterprise Edition), also known as Microsoft AD. In addition, you can establish a trust relationship between your Microsoft AD directory and your on-premises domain.

In this tutorial, we launch a WorkSpace that uses Microsoft AD. For tutorials that use the other options, see Launch a Virtual Desktop Using Amazon WorkSpaces.

Topics

- Before You Begin
- Step 1: Create a Microsoft AD Directory
- Step 2: Create a WorkSpace
- Step 3: Connect to the WorkSpace
- Next Steps

Before You Begin

- Amazon WorkSpaces is not available in every region. Verify the supported regions and select a region for your WorkSpaces. For more information about the supported regions, see Amazon WorkSpaces Pricing by AWS Region.
- When you launch a WorkSpace, you must select a WorkSpace bundle. A bundle is a combination of storage, compute, and software resources. For more information, see Amazon WorkSpaces Bundles.
- When you create a directory using AWS Directory Service or launch a WorkSpace, you must create or select a virtual private cloud configured with a public subnet and two private subnets. For more information, see Configure a VPC for Amazon WorkSpaces.

Step 1: Create a Microsoft AD Directory

Create a Microsoft AD directory. AWS Directory Service creates two directory servers, one in each of the private subnets of your VPC. Note that there are no users in the directory initially. You will add a user in the next step when you launch the WorkSpace.

To create a Microsoft AD directory

1. Open the Amazon WorkSpaces console at https://console.aws.amazon.com/workspaces/.

2. In the navigation pane, choose **Directories**.

3. Choose **Set up Directory**, **Create Microsoft AD**.

4. Configure the directory as follows:

    1. For **Organization name**, type a unique organization name for your directory (for example, my-demo-directory). This name must be at least four characters in length, consist of only alphanumeric characters and hyphens (-), and begin or end with a character other than a hyphen.

    2. For **Directory DNS**, type the fully-qualified name for the directory (for example, workspaces.demo.com).

    3. For **NetBIOS name**, type a short name for the directory (for example, workspaces).

4. For **Admin password** and **Confirm password**, type a password for the directory administrator account. For more information about the password requirements, see How to Create a Microsoft AD Directory in the *AWS Directory Service Administration Guide*.

5. (Optional) For **Description**, type a description for the directory.

6. For **VPC**, select the VPC that you created.

7. For **Subnets**, select the two private subnets (with the CIDR blocks 10.0.1.0/24 and 10.0.2.0/24).

8. Choose **Next Step**.

5. Choose **Create Microsoft AD**.

6. Choose **Done**. The initial status of the directory is Creating. When directory creation is complete, the status is Active.

Step 2: Create a WorkSpace

Now that you have created a Microsoft AD directory, you are ready to create a WorkSpace.

To create a WorkSpace

1. Open the Amazon WorkSpaces console at https://console.aws.amazon.com/workspaces/.

2. In the navigation pane, choose **WorkSpaces**.

3. Choose **Launch WorkSpaces**.

4. On the **Select a Directory** page, choose the directory that you created, and then choose **Next Step**. Amazon WorkSpaces registers your directory.

5. On the **Identify Users** page, add a new user to your directory as follows:

   1. Complete **Username**, **First Name**, **Last Name**, and **Email**. Use an email address that you have access to.

   2. Choose **Create Users**.

   3. Choose **Next Step**.

6. On the **Select Bundle** page, select a bundle and then choose **Next Step**.

7. On the **WorkSpaces Configuration** page, choose a running mode and then choose **Next Step**.

8. On the **Review & Launch WorkSpaces** page, choose **Launch WorkSpaces**. The initial status of the WorkSpace is PENDING. When the launch is complete, the status is AVAILABLE and an invitation is sent to the email address that you specified for the user.

Step 3: Connect to the WorkSpace

After you receive the invitation email, you can connect to your WorkSpace using the client of your choice. After you sign in, the client displays the WorkSpace desktop.

To connect to the WorkSpace

1. Open the link in the invitation email. When prompted, specify a password and activate the user. Remember this password as you will need it to sign in to your WorkSpace. **Note**
   Passwords are case-sensitive and must be between 8 and 64 characters in length, inclusive. Passwords must contain at least one character from three of the following categories: lowercase letters (a-z), uppercase letters (A-Z), numbers (0-9), and ~!@#$%^&*_-+=`|\(){}[]:;"'<>,.?/.

2. When prompted, download one of the client applications or launch Web Access.

   If you aren't prompted and you haven't installed a client application already, open http://clients. amazonworkspaces.com/ and follow the directions.

3. Start the client, enter the registration code from the invitation email, and choose **Register**.

4. When prompted to sign in, type the username and password for the user, and then choose **Sign In**.

5. (Optional) When prompted to save your credentials, choose **Yes**.

Next Steps

You can continue to customize the WorkSpace that you just created. For example, you can install software and then create a custom bundle from your WorkSpace. If you are finished with your WorkSpace, you can delete it. For more information, see the following documentation.

- Create a Custom WorkSpaces Bundle
- Administer Your WorkSpaces
- Manage Directories for Amazon WorkSpaces
- Delete a WorkSpace

Launch a WorkSpace Using Simple AD

Amazon WorkSpaces enables you to provision virtual, cloud-based Microsoft Windows desktops for your users, known as *WorkSpaces*.

Amazon WorkSpaces uses directories to store and manage information for your WorkSpaces and users. For your directory, you can choose from Simple AD, AD Connector, or AWS Directory Service for Microsoft Active Directory (Enterprise Edition), also known as Microsoft AD. In addition, you can establish a trust relationship between your Microsoft AD directory and your on-premises domain.

In this tutorial, we launch a WorkSpace that uses Simple AD. For tutorials that use the other options, see Launch a Virtual Desktop Using Amazon WorkSpaces.

Topics

- Before You Begin
- Step 1: Create a Simple AD Directory
- Step 2: Create a WorkSpace
- Step 3: Connect to the WorkSpace
- Next Steps

Before You Begin

- Simple AD is not available in every region. Verify the supported regions and select a region for your Simple AD directory. For more information about the supported regions, see the **Simple AD** table under AWS Directory Service.
- Amazon WorkSpaces is not available in every region. Verify the supported regions and select a region for your WorkSpaces. For more information about the supported regions, see Amazon WorkSpaces Pricing by AWS Region.
- When you launch a WorkSpace, you must select a WorkSpace bundle. A bundle is a combination of storage, compute, and software resources. For more information, see Amazon WorkSpaces Bundles.
- When you create a directory using AWS Directory Service or launch a WorkSpace, you must create or select a virtual private cloud configured with a public subnet and two private subnets. For more information, see Configure a VPC for Amazon WorkSpaces.

Step 1: Create a Simple AD Directory

Create a Simple AD directory. AWS Directory Service creates two directory servers, one in each of the private subnets of your VPC. Note that there are no users in the directory initially. You will add a user in the next step when you create the WorkSpace.

To create a Simple AD directory

1. Open the Amazon WorkSpaces console at https://console.aws.amazon.com/workspaces/.

2. In the navigation pane, choose **Directories**.

3. Choose **Set up Directory**, **Create Simple AD**.

4. Configure the directory as follows:

   1. For **Organization name**, type a unique organization name for your directory (for example, my-example-directory). This name must be at least four characters in length, consist of only alphanumeric characters and hyphens (-), and begin or end with a character other than a hyphen.

   2. For **Directory DNS**, type the fully-qualified name for the directory (for example, example.com).

   3. For **NetBIOS name**, type a short name for the directory (for example, example).

4. For **Admin password** and **Confirm password**, type a password for the directory administrator account. For more information about the password requirements, see How to Create a Microsoft AD Directory in the *AWS Directory Service Administration Guide*.

5. (Optional) For **Description**, type a description for the directory.

6. Keep **Directory size** as **Small**.

7. For **VPC**, select the VPC that you created.

8. For **Subnets**, select the two private subnets (with the CIDR blocks `10.0.1.0/24` and `10.0.2.0/24`).

9. Choose **Next Step**.

5. Choose **Create Simple AD**.

6. Choose **Done**. The initial status of the directory is `Requested` and then `Creating`. When directory creation is complete, the status is `Active`.

Directory Creation

Amazon WorkSpaces completes the following tasks on your behalf:

- Creates an IAM role to allow the Amazon WorkSpaces service to create elastic network interfaces and list your Amazon WorkSpaces directories. This role has the name `workspaces_DefaultRole`.
- Sets up a Simple AD directory in the VPC that is used to store user and WorkSpace information. The directory has an administrator account with the user name Administrator and the specified password.
- Creates two security groups, one for directory controllers and another for WorkSpaces in the directory.

Step 2: Create a WorkSpace

Now you are ready to launch the WorkSpace.

To create a WorkSpace for a user

1. Open the Amazon WorkSpaces console at https://console.aws.amazon.com/workspaces/.

2. In the navigation pane, choose **WorkSpaces**.

3. Choose **Launch WorkSpaces**.

4. On the **Select a Directory** page, do the following:

   1. For **Directory**, choose the directory that you created.

   2. For **Enable Amazon WorkDocs**, choose **Yes**. **Note**
   This option is available only if Amazon WorkDocs is available in the selected region.

   3. Choose **Next**. Amazon WorkSpaces registers your Simple AD directory.

5. On the **Identify Users** page, add a new user to your directory as follows:

   1. Complete **Username**, **First Name**, **Last Name**, and **Email**. Use an email address that you have access to.

   2. Choose **Create Users**.

   3. Choose **Next Step**.

6. On the **Select Bundle** page, select a bundle and then choose **Next Step**.

7. On the **WorkSpaces Configuration** page, choose a running mode and then choose **Next Step**.

8. On the **Review & Launch WorkSpaces** page, choose **Launch WorkSpaces**. The initial status of the WorkSpace is `PENDING`. When the launch is complete, the status is `AVAILABLE` and an invitation is sent to the email address that you specified for the user.

Step 3: Connect to the WorkSpace

After you receive the invitation email, you can connect to your WorkSpace using the client of your choice. After you sign in, the client displays the WorkSpace desktop.

To connect to the WorkSpace

1. Open the link in the invitation email. When prompted, type a password and activate the user. Remember this password as you will need it to sign in to your WorkSpace. **Note**
   Passwords are case-sensitive and must be between 8 and 64 characters in length, inclusive. Passwords must contain at least one character from three of the following categories: lowercase letters (a-z), uppercase letters (A-Z), numbers (0-9), and ~!@#$%^&*_-+=`|\(){}[]:;"'<>,.?/.

2. When prompted, download one of the client applications or launch Web Access.

   If you aren't prompted and you haven't installed a client application already, open http://clients.amazonworkspaces.com/ and follow the directions.

3. Start the client, enter the registration code from the invitation email, and choose **Register**.

4. When prompted to sign in, type the username and password for the user, and then choose **Sign In**.

5. (Optional) When prompted to save your credentials, choose **Yes**.

Next Steps

You can continue to customize the WorkSpace that you just created. For example, you can install software and then create a custom bundle from your WorkSpace. If you are finished with your WorkSpace, you can delete it. For more information, see the following documentation.

- Create a Custom WorkSpaces Bundle
- Administer Your WorkSpaces
- Manage Directories for Amazon WorkSpaces
- Delete a WorkSpace

Launch a WorkSpace Using AD Connector

Amazon WorkSpaces enables you to provision virtual, cloud-based Microsoft Windows desktops for your users, known as *WorkSpaces*.

Amazon WorkSpaces uses directories to store and manage information for your WorkSpaces and users. For your directory, you can choose from Simple AD, AD Connector, or AWS Directory Service for Microsoft Active Directory (Enterprise Edition), also known as Microsoft AD. In addition, you can establish a trust relationship between your Microsoft AD directory and your on-premises domain.

In this tutorial, we launch a WorkSpace that uses AD Connector. For tutorials that use the other options, see Launch a Virtual Desktop Using Amazon WorkSpaces.

Topics

- Before You Begin
- Step 1: Create an AD Connector
- Step 2: Create a WorkSpace
- Step 3: Connect to the WorkSpace
- Next Steps

Before You Begin

- Amazon WorkSpaces is not available in every region. Verify the supported regions and select a region for your WorkSpaces. For more information about the supported regions, see Amazon WorkSpaces Pricing by AWS Region.
- When you launch a WorkSpace, you must select a WorkSpace bundle. A bundle is a combination of storage, compute, and software resources. For more information, see Amazon WorkSpaces Bundles.
- Create a virtual private cloud with at least two private subnets. The VPC must be connected to your on-premises network through a virtual private network (VPN) connection or AWS Direct Connect. For more information, see AD Connector Prerequisites in the *AWS Directory Service Administration Guide*.
- Provide access to the Internet from the WorkSpace. For more information, see Provide Internet Access from Your WorkSpace.

Step 1: Create an AD Connector

To create an AD connector

1. Open the Amazon WorkSpaces console at https://console.aws.amazon.com/workspaces/.

2. In the navigation pane, choose **Directories**.

3. Choose **Set up Directory**, **Create AD Connector**.

4. For **Organization name**, type a unique organization name for your directory (for example, my-example-directory). This name must be at least four characters in length, consist of only alphanumeric characters and hyphens (-), and begin or end with a character other than a hyphen.

5. For **Connected directory DNS**, type the fully-qualified name of your on-premises directory (for example, example.com).

6. For **Connected directory NetBIOS name**, type the short name of your on-premises directory (for example, example).

7. For **Connector account username**, type the user name of a user in your on-premises directory. The user must have permissions to read users and groups, create computer objects, and join computers to the domain.

8. For **Connector account password** and **Confirm password**, type the password for the on-premises user account.

9. For **DNS address**, type the IP address of at least one DNS server in your on-premises directory.

10. (Optional) For **Description**, type a description for the directory.

11. Keep **Size** as **Small**.

12. For **VPC**, select your VPC.

13. For **Subnets**, select your subnets. The DNS servers that you specified must be accessible from each subnet.

14. Choose **Next Step**.

15. Choose **Create AD Connector**. It takes several minutes for your directory to be connected. The initial status of the directory is `Requested` and then `Creating`. When directory creation is complete, the status is `Active`.

Step 2: Create a WorkSpace

Now you are ready to launch WorkSpaces for one or more users in your on-premises directory.

To launch a WorkSpace for an existing user

1. Open the Amazon WorkSpaces console at https://console.aws.amazon.com/workspaces/.

2. In the navigation pane, choose **WorkSpaces**.

3. Choose **Launch WorkSpaces**.

4. For **Directory**, choose the directory that you created.

5. (Optional) If this is the first time you have launched a WorkSpace in this directory, and Amazon WorkDocs is supported in the region, you can enable or disable Amazon WorkDocs for all users in the directory. For more information, see Amazon WorkDocs Sync Client Help in the *Amazon WorkDocs Administration Guide*.

6. Choose **Next**. Amazon WorkSpaces registers your AD Connector.

7. Select one or more existing users from your on-premises directory. Do not add new users to an on-premises directory through the Amazon WorkSpaces console.

   To find users to select, you can type all or part of the user's name and choose **Search** or choose **Show All Users**. Note that you cannot select a user that does not have an email address.

   After you select the users, choose **Add Selected** and then choose **Next Step**.

8. Under **Select Bundle**, choose the default WorkSpace bundle to be used for the WorkSpaces. Under **Assign WorkSpace Bundles**, you can choose a different the bundle for an individual WorkSpace if needed. When you have finished, choose **Next Step**.

9. Choose a running mode for your WorkSpaces and then choose **Next Step**. For more information, see Manage the WorkSpace Running Mode.

10. Choose **Launch WorkSpaces**. The initial status of the WorkSpace is `PENDING`. When the launch is complete, the status is `AVAILABLE`.

11. Send invitations to the email address for each user. For more information, see Send an Invitation Email.

Step 3: Connect to the WorkSpace

You can connect to your WorkSpace using the client of your choice. After you sign in, the client displays the WorkSpace desktop.

To connect to the WorkSpace

1. Open the link in the invitation email.

2. When prompted, download one of the client applications or launch Web Access.

   If you aren't prompted and you haven't installed a client application already, open http://clients. amazonworkspaces.com/ and follow the directions.

3. Start the client, enter the registration code from the invitation email, and choose **Register**.

4. When prompted to sign in, type the username and password for the user, and then choose **Sign In**.

5. (Optional) When prompted to save your credentials, choose **Yes**.

Next Steps

You can continue to customize the WorkSpace that you just created. For example, you can install software and then create a custom bundle from your WorkSpace. If you are finished with your WorkSpace, you can delete it. For more information, see the following documentation.

- Create a Custom WorkSpaces Bundle
- Administer Your WorkSpaces
- Manage Directories for Amazon WorkSpaces
- Delete a WorkSpace

Launch a WorkSpace Using a Trusted Domain

Amazon WorkSpaces enables you to provision virtual, cloud-based Microsoft Windows desktops for your users, known as *WorkSpaces*.

Amazon WorkSpaces uses directories to store and manage information for your WorkSpaces and users. For your directory, you can choose from Simple AD, AD Connector, or AWS Directory Service for Microsoft Active Directory (Enterprise Edition), also known as Microsoft AD. In addition, you can establish a trust relationship between your Microsoft AD directory and your on-premises domain.

In this tutorial, we launch a WorkSpace that uses a trust relationship. For tutorials that use the other options, see Launch a Virtual Desktop Using Amazon WorkSpaces.

Topics

- Before You Begin
- Step 1: Establish a Trust Relationship
- Step 2: Create a WorkSpace
- Step 3: Connect to the WorkSpace
- Next Steps

Before You Begin

- Amazon WorkSpaces is not available in every region. Verify the supported regions and select a region for your WorkSpaces. For more information about the supported regions, see Amazon WorkSpaces Pricing by AWS Region.
- When you launch a WorkSpace, you must select a WorkSpace bundle. A bundle is a combination of storage, compute, and software resources. For more information, see Amazon WorkSpaces Bundles.

Step 1: Establish a Trust Relationship

To set up the trust relationship

1. Set up Microsoft AD in your virtual private cloud (VPC). For more information, see How to Create a Microsoft AD directory in the *AWS Directory Service Administration Guide*.

2. Create a trust relationship between your Microsoft AD and your on-premises domain. Ensure that the trust is configured as a two-way trust. For more information, see Tutorial: Create a Trust Relationship Between Your Microsoft AD and Your On-Premises Domain in the *AWS Directory Service Administration Guide*.

Step 2: Create a WorkSpace

After you establish a trust relationship between your AWS Microsoft AD and your on-premises Microsoft Active Directory domain, you can provision WorkSpaces for users in the on-premises domain.

Note that you must ensure that GPO settings are replicated across domains before you can apply them to Amazon WorkSpaces.

To launch workspaces for users in a trusted on-premises domain

1. Open the Amazon WorkSpaces console at https://console.aws.amazon.com/workspaces/.

2. In the navigation pane, choose **WorkSpaces**.

3. Choose **Launch WorkSpaces**.

4. On the **Select a Directory** page, choose the directory that you just registered and then choose **Next Step**.

5. On the **Identify Users** page, do the following:

   1. For **Select trust from forest**, select the trust relationship that you created.

   2. Select the users from the on-premises domain and then choose **Add Selected**.

   3. Choose **Next Step**.

6. Select the bundle to be used for the WorkSpaces and then choose **Next Step**.

7. Choose the running mode, choose the encryption settings, and configure any tags. When you are finished, choose **Next Step**.

8. Choose **Launch WorkSpaces**. Note that it can take up to 20 minutes for the WorkSpaces to become available, and up to 40 minutes if encryption is enabled. The initial status of the WorkSpace is `PENDING`. When the launch is complete, the status is `AVAILABLE` and an invitation is sent to the email address for each user.

Step 3: Connect to the WorkSpace

After you receive the invitation email, you can connect to your WorkSpace. Users can enter their user names as *username*, *corp\username*, or *corp.example.com\username*).

To connect to the WorkSpace

1. Open the link in the invitation email. When prompted, type a password and activate the user. Remember this password as you will need it to sign in to your WorkSpace. **Note**
Passwords are case-sensitive and must be between 8 and 64 characters in length, inclusive. Passwords must contain at least one character from three of the following categories: lowercase letters (a-z), uppercase letters (A-Z), numbers (0-9), and ~!@#$%^&*_-+='|\(){}[]:;"'<>,.?/.

2. When prompted, download one of the client applications or launch Web Access.

   If you aren't prompted and you haven't installed a client application already, open http://clients. amazonworkspaces.com/ and follow the directions.

3. Start the client, enter the registration code from the invitation email, and choose **Register**.

4. When prompted to sign in, type the username and password for the user, and then choose **Sign In**.

5. (Optional) When prompted to save your credentials, choose **Yes**.

Next Steps

You can continue to customize the WorkSpace that you just created. For example, you can install software and then create a custom bundle from your WorkSpace. If you are finished with your WorkSpace, you can delete it. For more information, see the following documentation.

- Create a Custom WorkSpaces Bundle
- Administer Your WorkSpaces
- Manage Directories for Amazon WorkSpaces
- Delete a WorkSpace

Administer Your WorkSpaces

You can administer your WorkSpaces using the Amazon WorkSpaces console.

Amazon WorkSpaces schedules maintenance for your WorkSpaces. During the maintenance window, we download and install important updates. For AlwaysOn WorkSpaces, the maintenance window is each Sunday morning, from 00:00 to 04:00 in the time zone of the AWS region for the WorkSpace. During this time, your WorkSpaces might be unavailable. For AutoStop WorkSpaces, you can enable maintenance mode or install updates manually. For more information, see Set Maintenance Mode.

Topics

- Manage WorkSpaces Users
- Manage the WorkSpace Running Mode
- Modify a WorkSpace
- Tag a WorkSpace
- Encrypt a WorkSpace
- Reboot a WorkSpace
- Rebuild a WorkSpace
- Delete a WorkSpace
- Upgrade Windows 10 BYOL WorkSpaces

Manage WorkSpaces Users

Each WorkSpace is assigned to a single user and cannot be shared by multiple users. Whenever you launch a WorkSpace, you must assign it to a user that does not already have a WorkSpace.

As an administrator for Amazon WorkSpaces, you can use the Amazon WorkSpaces console to perform the following tasks to manage WorkSpaces users.

Edit User Information

You can use the Amazon WorkSpaces console to edit the user information for a WorkSpace.

Note
This feature is available only if you use Microsoft AD or Simple AD. If you use Microsoft Active Directory through AD Connector or a trust relationship, you can manage users and groups using Active Directory Users and Computers.

To edit user information

1. Open the Amazon WorkSpaces console at https://console.aws.amazon.com/workspaces/.

2. In the navigation pane, choose **WorkSpaces**.

3. Select a user and choose **Actions, Edit User**.

4. Update **First Name**, **Last Name**, and **Email** as needed.

5. Choose **Update**.

Send an Invitation Email

You can send an invitation email to a user manually if needed.

To resend an invitation email

1. Open the Amazon WorkSpaces console at https://console.aws.amazon.com/workspaces/.

2. In the navigation pane, choose **WorkSpaces**.

3. Select the user to send the invitation to and choose **Actions, Invite User**.

4. Copy the email body text and paste it into an email to the user using your own email application. You can modify the body text if desired. When the invitation email is ready, send it to the user.

Manage the WorkSpace Running Mode

The *running mode* of a WorkSpaces determines its immediate availability and how you pay for it. You can choose between the following running modes when you create the WorkSpace:

- **AlwaysOn** — Use when paying a fixed monthly fee for unlimited usage of your WorkSpaces. This mode is best for users who use their WorkSpace full time as their primary desktop.

- **AutoStop** — Use when paying for your WorkSpaces by the hour. With this mode, your WorkSpaces stop after a specified period of inactivity and the state of apps and data is saved. To set the automatic stop time, use **AutoStop Time (hours)**.

  When possible, the state of the desktop is saved to the root volume of the WorkSpace. The WorkSpace resumes when a user logs in, and all open documents and running programs return to their saved state.

For more information, see Amazon WorkSpaces Pricing.

Modify the Running Mode

You can switch between running modes at any time.

To modify the running mode of a WorkSpace

1. Open the Amazon WorkSpaces console at https://console.aws.amazon.com/workspaces/.

2. In the navigation pane, choose **WorkSpaces**.

3. Select the WorkSpaces to modify and choose **Actions, Modify Running Mode Properties**.

4. Select the new running mode, **AlwaysOn** or **AutoStop**, and then choose **Modify**.

Stop and Start an AutoStop WorkSpace

When your AutoStop WorkSpaces are not in use, they are automatically stopped after a specified period of inactivity, and hourly metering is suspended. To further optimize costs, you can suspend the hourly charges associated with AutoStop WorkSpaces. The WorkSpace is stopped and all apps and data saved for the next time a user logs in to the WorkSpace.

When a user reconnects to a stopped WorkSpace, it resumes from where it left off, typically in under 90 seconds.

You can restart AutoStop WorkSpaces that are available or in an error state.

To stop an AutoStop WorkSpace

1. Open the Amazon WorkSpaces console at https://console.aws.amazon.com/workspaces/.

2. In the navigation pane, choose **WorkSpaces**.

3. Select the WorkSpaces to be stopped and choose **Actions, Stop WorkSpaces**.

4. When prompted for confirmation, choose **Stop**.

To start an AutoStop WorkSpace

1. Open the Amazon WorkSpaces console at https://console.aws.amazon.com/workspaces/.

2. In the navigation pane, choose **WorkSpaces**.

3. Select the WorkSpaces to be started and choose **Actions, Start WorkSpaces**.

4. When prompted for confirmation, choose **Start**.

To remove the fixed infrastructure costs associated with AutoStop WorkSpaces, remove the WorkSpace from your account. For more information, see Delete a WorkSpace.

Set Maintenance Mode

If you enable maintenance mode for your AutoStop WorkSpaces, they are started automatically one time a month in order to download and install important service, security, and Windows updates. Unless the updates are delayed, we schedule the maintenance window for the third Monday of the month from 00:00 to 05:00 in the time zone of the Region for the WorkSpace.

After you enable maintenance mode, ensure that your WorkSpaces are in the stopped state between 00:00 and 02:00 of the maintenance window. Otherwise, they are not maintained automatically.

If you manage updates to your WorkSpaces on a regular basis, you can disable maintenance mode.

To set maintenance mode

1. Open the Amazon WorkSpaces console at https://console.aws.amazon.com/workspaces/.

2. In the navigation pane, choose **Directories**.

3. Select your directory, and choose **Actions, Update Details**.

4. Expand **Maintenance Mode**.

5. To enable automatic updates, choose **Enabled**. If you manage updates manually, choose **Disabled**.

6. Choose **Update and Exit**.

Modify a WorkSpace

You can increase the size of the root and user volumes for a WorkSpace, up to 1000 GB each. You can expand these volumes whether they are encrypted or unencrypted. You can request a volume expansion once in a 24-hour period. To ensure that your data is preserved, you cannot decrease the size of the root or user volumes after you launch a WorkSpace.

You can switch a WorkSpace between Value, Standard, Performance, and Power bundles. When you request a bundle change, Amazon WorkSpaces reboots the WorkSpace using the new bundle. Amazon WorkSpaces preserves the operating system, applications, data, and storage settings for the WorkSpace. You can request a larger bundle one time in a 24-hour period or a smaller bundle one time in 30 days. For a newly launched WorkSpace, you must wait 24 hours before requesting a larger bundle.

To modify the configuration of a WorkSpace

1. Open the Amazon WorkSpaces console at https://console.aws.amazon.com/workspaces/.

2. In the navigation pane, choose **WorkSpaces**.

3. Select the WorkSpace and choose **Actions**, **Modify WorkSpace**.

4. To increase the size of the root volume or user volume, choose **Modify Volume Sizes** and type the new values.

5. To change the bundle, choose **Change Compute Type** and select the new bundle type.

6. Choose **Modify**.

Tag a WorkSpace

You can organize and manage your WorkSpaces by assigning your own metadata to each WorkSpace in the form of *tags*. You specify a *key* and a *value* for each tag. A key can be a general category, such as "project," "owner," or "environment," with specific associated values. Using tags is a simple yet powerful way to manage AWS resources and organize data, including billing data.

You can apply tags to a WorkSpace when you launch it or apply them to the WorkSpace later on. Each tag automatically applies to all WAM applications and WAM related service charges for the WorkSpace. Tags added to existing WorkSpaces appear in your cost allocation report on the first of the following month for WorkSpaces renewed in that month. For more information, see Setting Up Your Monthly Cost Allocation Report.

Tag Restrictions

- The maximum number of tags per WorkSpace is 50.
- The maximum key length is 127 characters.
- The maximum value length is 255 characters.
- Tag keys and values are both case-sensitive.
- Tags with a prefix of "aws:" or "aws:workspaces:" cannot be used. These prefixes are reserved for AWS and WorkSpaces, respectively. Tags with these prefixes cannot be edited or deleted.

To update the tags for an existing WorkSpace

1. Open the Amazon WorkSpaces console at https://console.aws.amazon.com/workspaces/.

2. In the navigation pane, choose **WorkSpaces**.

3. Select the WorkSpace and choose **Actions, Manage Tags**.

4. Do one or more of the following:

    1. To update a tag, edit the values of **Key** and **Value**.

    2. To add a tag, choose **Add Tag** and then edit the values of **Key** and **Value**.

    3. To delete a tag, choose the delete icon (X) next to the tag.

5. When you are finished updating tags, choose **Save**.

Encrypt a WorkSpace

Amazon WorkSpaces is integrated with the AWS Key Management Service (AWS KMS). This enables you to encrypt storage volumes of WorkSpaces using customer master keys (CMK). When you launch a WorkSpace, you have the option to encrypt the root volume (C: drive) and the user volume (D: drive). This ensures that the data stored at rest, disk I/O to the volume, and snapshots created from the volumes are all encrypted.

Prerequisites

You need an AWS KMS CMK before you can begin the encryption process.

The first time you launch a WorkSpace from the Amazon WorkSpaces console in a region, a default CMK is created for you automatically. You can select this key to encrypt the user and root volumes of your WorkSpace.

Alternately, you can select a CMK that you created using AWS KMS. For more information about creating keys, see Creating Keys in the *AWS Key Management Service Developer Guide*. For more information about creating keys using the AWS KMS API, see Working With Keys in the *AWS Key Management Service Developer Guide*.

You must meet the following requirements to use an AWS KMS CMK to encrypt your WorkSpaces:

- The key must be enabled.
- You must have the correct permissions and policies associated with the key. For more information, see IAM Permissions and Roles for Encryption.

Limits

- Creating a custom image from an encrypted WorkSpace is not supported.
- Disabling encryption for an encrypted WorkSpace is not currently supported.
- WorkSpaces launched with root volume encryption enabled might take up to an hour to provision.
- To reboot or rebuild an encrypted WorkSpace, first make sure that the AWS KMS CMK is enabled; otherwise, the WorkSpace becomes unusable.

Encrypting WorkSpaces

To encrypt a WorkSpace

1. Open the Amazon WorkSpaces console at https://console.aws.amazon.com/workspaces/.
2. Choose **Launch WorkSpaces** and complete the first three steps.
3. For the **WorkSpaces Configuration** step, do the following:
   1. Select the volumes to encrypt: **Root Volume**, **User Volume**, or both volumes.
   2. For **Encryption Key**, choose your AWS KMS CMK.
   3. Choose **Next Step**.
4. Choose **Launch WorkSpaces**.

Viewing Encrypted WorkSpaces

To see which WorkSpaces and volumes have been encrypted from the Amazon WorkSpaces console, choose **WorkSpaces** from the navigation bar on the left. The **Volume Encryption** column shows whether each WorkSpace has encryption enabled or disabled. To see which specific volumes have been encrypted, expand the WorkSpace entry to see the **Encrypted Volumes** field.

IAM Permissions and Roles for Encryption

Amazon WorkSpaces encryption privileges require limited AWS KMS access on a given key for the IAM user who launches encrypted WorkSpaces. The following is a sample key policy that can be used. This policy enables you to separate the principals that can manage the AWS KMS CMK from those that can use it. The account ID and IAM user name must be modified to match your account.

The first statement matches the default AWS KMS key policy. The second and third statements define which AWS principals can manage and use the key, respectively. The fourth statement enables AWS services that are integrated with AWS KMS to use the key on behalf of the specified principal. This statement enables AWS services to create and manage grants. The condition uses a context key that is set only for AWS KMS calls made by AWS services on behalf of the customers.

```
1  {
2    "Version": "2012-10-17",
3    "Statement": [
4      {
5        "Effect": "Allow",
6        "Principal": {"AWS": "arn:aws:iam::123456789012:root"},
7        "Action": "kms:*",
8        "Resource": "*"
9      },
10     {
11       "Effect": "Allow",
12       "Principal": {"AWS": "arn:aws:iam::123456789012:user/Alice"},
13       "Action": [
14         "kms:Create*",
15         "kms:Describe*",
16         "kms:Enable*",
17         "kms:List*",
18         "kms:Put*",
19         "kms:Update*",
20         "kms:Revoke*",
21         "kms:Disable*",
22         "kms:Get*",
23         "kms:Delete*"
24       ],
25       "Resource": "*"
26     },
27     {
28       "Effect": "Allow",
29       "Principal": {"AWS": "arn:aws:iam::123456789012:user/Alice"},
30       "Action": [
31         "kms:Encrypt",
32         "kms:Decrypt",
33         "kms:ReEncrypt",
34         "kms:GenerateDataKey*",
35         "kms:DescribeKey"
36       ],
37       "Resource": "*"
38     },
39     {
40       "Effect": "Allow",
41       "Principal": {"AWS": "arn:aws:iam::123456789012:user/Alice"},
42       "Action": [
43         "kms:CreateGrant",
```

```
44          "kms:ListGrants",
45          "kms:RevokeGrant"
46        ],
47        "Resource": "*",
48        "Condition": {"Bool": {"kms:GrantIsForAWSResource": "true"}}
49      }
50    ]
51 }
```

The IAM policy for a user or role that is encrypting a WorkSpace should include usage permissions on the CMK, as well as access to WorkSpaces. The following is a sample policy that can be attached to an IAM user to grant them WorkSpaces privileges.

```
1  {
2      "Version": "2012-10-17",
3      "Statement": [
4          {
5              "Effect": "Allow",
6              "Action": [
7                  "ds:*",
8                  "ds:DescribeDirectories",
9                  "workspaces:*",
10                 "workspaces:DescribeWorkspaceBundles",
11                 "wam:CreateWorkspaces",
12                 "wam:DescribeWorkspaceBundles",
13                 "wam:DescribeWorkspaceDirectories",
14                 "wam:DescribeWorkspaces",
15                 "wam:RebootWorkspaces",
16                 "wam:RebuildWorkspaces"
17             ],
18             "Resource": "*"
19         }
20     ]
21 }
```

The following is the IAM policy required by the user for using AWS KMS.

```
1  {
2      "Version": "2012-10-17",
3      "Statement": [
4          {
5              "Effect": "Allow",
6              "Action": [
7                  "kms:CreateGrant",
8                  "kms:Describe*",
9                  "kms:List*"
10             ],
11             "Resource": "*"
12         }
13     ]
14 }
```

Reboot a WorkSpace

Occasionally, you may find it necessary to reboot a WorkSpace manually. Rebooting a WorkSpace performs a shutdown and restart of the WorkSpace. The user data, operating system, and system settings are not affected.

To reboot a WorkSpace

1. Open the Amazon WorkSpaces console at https://console.aws.amazon.com/workspaces/.

2. In the navigation pane, choose **WorkSpaces**.

3. Select the WorkSpaces to be rebooted and choose **Actions**, **Reboot WorkSpaces**.

4. When prompted for confirmation, choose **Reboot WorkSpaces**.

Rebuild a WorkSpace

If needed, you can rebuild the operating system of a WorkSpace to its original state. Rebuilding a WorkSpace causes the following to occur:

- The system is restored to the most recent image of the bundle that the WorkSpace is created from. Any applications that have been installed, or system settings that have been made after the WorkSpace was created are lost.
- The data drive (D drive) is recreated from the last automatic snapshot taken of the data drive. The current contents of the data drive is overwritten. Automatic snapshots of the data drive are taken every 12 hours, so the snapshot can be as much as 12 hours old.

To rebuild a WorkSpace

1. Open the Amazon WorkSpaces console at https://console.aws.amazon.com/workspaces/.

2. In the navigation pane, choose **WorkSpaces**.

3. Select the WorkSpace to be rebuilt and choose **Actions**, **Rebuild WorkSpace**.

4. When prompted for confirmation, choose **Rebuild WorkSpace**.

Delete a WorkSpace

When you are finished with a WorkSpace, you can delete it. You can also delete related resources.

Warning
This is a permanent action and cannot be undone. The WorkSpace user's data does not persist and is destroyed. For help with backing up user data, contact AWS Support.

To delete a WorkSpace

1. Open the Amazon WorkSpaces console at https://console.aws.amazon.com/workspaces/.

2. In the navigation pane, choose **WorkSpaces**.

3. Select your WorkSpace and choose **Actions**, **Remove WorkSpaces**.

4. When prompted for confirmation, choose **Remove WorkSpaces**. The status of the WorkSpace is set to `TERMINATING`. When the termination is complete, the status is set to `TERMINATED`.

5. (Optional) To delete any custom bundles and images that you are finished with, see Delete a Custom WorkSpaces Bundle.

6. (Optional) After you delete all WorkSpaces in a directory, you can delete the directory. For more information, see Delete the Directory for Your WorkSpaces.

7. (Optional) After you delete all resources in the virtual private cloud (VPC) for your directory, you can delete the VPC and release the Elastic IP address used for the NAT gateway.

Upgrade Windows 10 BYOL WorkSpaces

On your Windows 10 BYOL WorkSpaces, you can upgrade your Windows 10 WorkSpace to a newer version of Windows 10 using in-place upgrade. Follow the instructions in this topic to do so.

Note
This guidance applies only to Windows 10 BYOL WorkSpaces. WorkSpaces with the Windows 10 desktop experience are based on Windows Server 2016 and do not need regular OS release upgrades from Microsoft.

Prerequisites

- If you have deferred or paused Windows 10 upgrades using Group Policy or System Center Configuration Manager (SCCM), enable operating system upgrades for your Windows 10 WorkSpaces.
- If the WorkSpace is an AutoStop WorkSpace, change it to an AlwaysOn WorkSpace before the in-place upgrade process so that it won't be stopped automatically while updates are being applied. For more information, see Modify the Running Mode. To leave them set to AutoStop, change the AutoStop time to three hours or more while the upgrades take place.
- The in-place upgrade process re-creates the user profile by making a copy of a special profile named Default User (`C:\Users\Default`). To preserve custom Windows preferences and application settings stored in the Windows registry, modify `C:\Users\Default\NTUSER.DAT` on the WorkSpace before you perform the in-place upgrades.

To perform an in-place upgrade of Windows 10

1. Check the version of Windows currently running on the Windows 10 BYOL WorkSpaces that you are updating, and then reboot them.

2. Update the following Windows system registry keys to change the value data for **Enabled** from 0 to 1. These registry changes enable the in-place upgrade for the WorkSpace.

   You can do this manually. If you have multiple WorkSpaces to update, you can use Group Policy or SCCM to push a PowerShell script.

   - **HKEY_LOCAL_MACHINE\SOFTWARE\Amazon\WorkSpacesConfig\enable-inplace-upgrade.ps1**
   - **HKEY_LOCAL_MACHINE\SOFTWARE\Amazon\WorkSpacesConfig\upgrade-pvdrivers.ps1 Note**
     If these keys do not exist, reboot the WorkSpace. The keys should be added when the system is rebooted.

3. After saving the changes to the registry, reboot the WorkSpace again so that the changes are applied. **Note**
   After the reboot, logging into the WorkSpace creates a new user profile. You may see placeholder icons in the **Start** menu. This is automatically resolved after the in-place upgrade completes.

   [Optional check]: Confirm that the value data for the following key value is set to 1, which unblocks the WorkSpace for updating:

   HKEY_LOCAL_MACHINE\SOFTWARE\Amazon\WorkSpacesConfig\enable-inplace-upgrade.ps1\profileImagePathDeleted

4. Perform the in-place upgrade. You can use whichever method you like, such as SCCM, ISO, or Windows Update (WU). Depending on your original Windows 10 version and how many apps were installed, this can take 40-120 minutes.

5. After the update completes, confirm that the Windows version has been updated. **Note**
   If the in-place upgrade fails, Windows automatically rolls back to use the Windows 10 version that was in place before you started the upgrade. For more information about troubleshooting, see the Microsoft documentation.

[Optional check]: To confirm that the update scripts were successfully executed, verify that the value data for the following key value is set to 1.

HKEY_LOCAL_MACHINE\SOFTWARE\Amazon\WorkSpacesConfig\enable-inplace-upgrade.ps1\scriptExecutionComplete

After in-place upgrades, the `NTUSER.DAT` file of the user is regenerated and placed onto the C drive, so that you do not have to go through the above steps again for future Windows 10 in-place upgrades. WorkSpaces redirects the following shell folders to the D drive:

- `D:\Users\%USERNAME%\Downloads`
- `D:\Users\%USERNAME%\AppData\Roaming`
- `D:\Users\%USERNAME%\Desktop`
- `D:\Users\%USERNAME%\Favorites`
- `D:\Users\%USERNAME%\Music`
- `D:\Users\%USERNAME%\Pictures`
- `D:\Users\%USERNAME%\Videos`
- `D:\Users\%USERNAME%\Documents`

If you redirect the shell folders to other locations on your WorkSpaces, perform the necessary operations on WorkSpaces after the in-place upgrades.

Known Limitations

The `NTUSER.DAT` location change does not happen during WorkSpaces rebuilds. If you perform an in-place upgrade on a Windows 10 BYOL WorkSpace, and then rebuild it, the new WorkSpace uses the `NTUSER.DAT` on the D drive. Also, if your default bundle contains the image that is based on an earlier release of Windows 10, you need to perform the in-place upgrade again after the WorkSpace is rebuilt.

Troubleshooting

If you encounter any issues with the update, you can check the following to troubleshoot:

- Windows Logs, which are located, by default, in the following locations:

  `C:\Program Files\Amazon\WorkSpacesConfig\Logs\`

  `C:\Program Files\Amazon\WorkSpacesConfig\Logs\TRANSMITTED`

- Windows Event Viewer

  Windows Logs > Application > Source: Amazon WorkSpaces

- If, during the process, you see that some icon short-cuts on the desktop no longer work, it is because WorkSpaces moves any user profiles located on drive D to drive C to prepare for the upgrade. After the upgrade is completed, the short-cuts work as expected.

Update Your WorkSpace Registry Using a PowerShell Script

You can use the following sample PowerShell script to update the registry on your WorkSpaces to enable in-place upgrade. Follow the steps in the previous section, but use this script to update the registry on each WorkSpace.

```
1  # AWS WorkSpaces 2.13.18
2  # Enable In-Place Update Sample Scripts
3  # These registry keys and values will enable scripts to execute on next reboot of the WorkSpace.
4
5  $scriptlist = ("update-pvdrivers.ps1","enable-inplace-upgrade.ps1")
```

```
6 $wsConfigRegistryRoot="HKLM:\Software\Amazon\WorkSpacesConfig"
7 $Enabled = 1
8
9 foreach ($scriptName in $scriptlist)
10 {
11     $scriptRegKey = "$wsConfigRegistryRoot\$scriptName"
12     if (-not(Test-Path $scriptRegKey))
13     {
14         Write-Host "Registry key not found. Creating registry key '$scriptRegKey' with 'Update'
               enabled."
15         New-Item -Path $wsConfigRegistryRoot -Name $scriptName -ErrorAction SilentlyContinue |
               Out-Null
16         New-ItemProperty -Path $scriptRegKey -Name Enabled -PropertyType DWord -Value $Enabled |
               Out-Null
17         Write-Host "Value created. '$scriptRegKey' Enabled='$((Get-ItemProperty -Path
               $scriptRegKey).Enabled)'"
18     }
19     else
20     {
21         Write-Host "Registry key is already present with value '$scriptRegKey' Enabled='$((Get-
               ItemProperty -Path $scriptRegKey).Enabled)'"
22         if((Get-ItemProperty -Path $scriptRegKey).Enabled -ne $Enabled)
23         {
24             Set-ItemProperty -Path $scriptRegKey -Name Enabled -Value $Enabled
25             Write-Host "Value updated. '$scriptRegKey' Enabled='$((Get-ItemProperty -Path
                   $scriptRegKey).Enabled)'"
26         }
27     }
28 }
```

WorkSpace Bundles and Images

A *WorkSpace bundle* specifies the hardware and software for your WorkSpace. When you launch a WorkSpace, you select the bundle that meets your needs. For more information, see Amazon WorkSpaces Bundles.

You can create an image from a WorkSpace that you've customized, create a *custom WorkSpace bundle* from the image, and launch WorkSpaces from your custom bundle. By creating a custom bundle, you can ensure that the WorkSpaces for your users have everything that they need already installed. If you need to perform software updates or install additional software on your WorkSpaces, you can update your custom bundle and rebuild your WorkSpaces.

Topics

- Create a Custom WorkSpaces Bundle
- Update a Custom WorkSpaces Bundle
- Delete a Custom WorkSpaces Bundle
- Bring Your Own Windows Desktop Images

Create a Custom WorkSpaces Bundle

After you've launched a WorkSpace and customized it, you can create an image from the WorkSpace and then create a custom bundle from the image. You can specify this bundle when you launch new WorkSpaces to ensure that they have the same configuration and software as the WorkSpace you used to create the bundle.

Requirements

- All applications to be included in the image must be installed on the C:\ drive, or the user profile in D:\Users*username*. They must also be compatible with Microsoft Sysprep.
- The user profile must exist and its total size (files and data) must be less than 10 GB.
- The C:\ drive must have enough available space for the contents of the user profile, plus an additional 2 GB.
- All application services running on the WorkSpace must use a local system account instead of domain user credentials. For example, you cannot have a Microsoft SQL Server Express installation running with a domain user's credentials.
- The following components are required in an image; otherwise, the WorkSpaces you launch from the image will not function correctly:
  - PowerShell
  - Remote Desktop Services
  - AWS PV drivers
  - EC2Config or EC2Launch (Windows Server 2016)
  - [EC2Launch 1.2.0 or earlier] Windows Remote Management (WinRM)
  - Teradici PCoIP agents and drivers
  - STXHD agents and drivers
  - AWS and WorkSpaces certificates
  - Skylight agent

Best Practices

Before you create an image from a WorkSpace, do the following:

- Install all operating system and application updates on the WorkSpace.
- Delete cached data from the WorkSpace that shouldn't be included in the bundle (for example, browser history, cached files, and browser cookies).
- Delete configuration settings from the WorkSpace that shouldn't be included in the bundle (for example, email profiles).

To create a custom bundle

1. If you are still connected to the WorkSpace, disconnect.

2. Open the Amazon WorkSpaces console at https://console.aws.amazon.com/workspaces/.

3. In the navigation pane, choose **WorkSpaces**.

4. Select the WorkSpace and choose **Actions, Create Image**.

5. Type an image name and a description that will help you identify the image, and then choose **Create Image**. The WorkSpace is unavailable while the image is being created.

6. In the navigation pane, choose **Images**. The image is complete when the status changes to **Available**.

7. Select the image and choose **Actions, Create Bundle**.

8. Type a bundle name and a description, select a hardware type, and choose **Create Bundle**.

Image Creation

When you create an image, the entire contents of the C:\ drive are included. The entire contents of the user profile in D:\Users*username* are included except for the following:

- Contacts
- Downloads
- Music
- Pictures
- Saved games
- Videos
- Podcasts
- Virtual machines
- .virtualbox
- Tracing
- appdata\local\temp
- appdata\roaming\apple computer\mobilesync\
- appdata\roaming\apple computer\logs\
- appdata\roaming\apple computer\itunes\iphone software updates\
- appdata\roaming\macromedia\flash player\macromedia.com\support\flashplayer\sys\
- appdata\roaming\macromedia\flash player\#sharedobjects\
- appdata\roaming\adobe\flash player\assetcache\
- appdata\roaming\microsoft\windows\recent\
- appdata\roaming\microsoft\office\recent\
- appdata\roaming\microsoft office\live meeting
- appdata\roaming\microsoft shared\livemeeting shared\
- appdata\roaming\mozilla\firefox\crash reports\
- appdata\roaming\mcafee\common framework\
- appdata\local\microsoft\feeds cache
- appdata\local\microsoft\windows\temporary internet files\
- appdata\local\microsoft\windows\history\
- appdata\local\microsoft\internet explorer\domstore\
- appdata\local\microsoft\internet explorer\imagestore\
- appdata\locallow\microsoft\internet explorer\iconcache\
- appdata\locallow\microsoft\internet explorer\domstore\
- appdata\locallow\microsoft\internet explorer\imagestore\
- appdata\local\microsoft\internet explorer\recovery\
- appdata\local\mozilla\firefox\profiles\

Update a Custom WorkSpaces Bundle

You can update an existing custom WorkSpaces bundle by modifying a WorkSpace based on the bundle, creating an image from the WorkSpace, and updating the bundle with the new image. You can launch new WorkSpaces using the updated bundle. To update existing WorkSpaces that are based on the bundle, rebuild the WorkSpace.

To update a bundle

1. Connect to a WorkSpace that is based on the bundle and make any changes. For example, you can apply the latest operating system and application patches and install additional applications.

   Alternatively, you can create a WorkSpace with the same base software package (Plus or Standard) as the image used to create the bundle and make changes.

2. Open the Amazon WorkSpaces console at https://console.aws.amazon.com/workspaces/.

3. In the navigation pane, choose **WorkSpaces**.

4. Select the WorkSpace and choose **Actions**, **Create Image**.

5. Type an image name and a description, and then choose **Create Image**. The WorkSpace is unavailable while the image is being created.

6. In the navigation pane, choose **Bundles**.

7. Select the bundle and choose **Actions**, **Update Bundle**.

8. For **Update WorkSpace Bundle**, select the image that you created and choose **Update Bundle**.

9. (Optional) Rebuild the existing WorkSpaces based on the bundle. For more information, see Rebuild a WorkSpace.

Delete a Custom WorkSpaces Bundle

You can delete unused custom bundles as needed. If you delete a bundle that is being used by a WorkSpace, the bundle is placed in a delete queue and will be deleted after all WorkSpaces based on the bundle have been deleted.

To delete a bundle

1. Open the Amazon WorkSpaces console at https://console.aws.amazon.com/workspaces/.

2. In the navigation pane, choose **Bundles**.

3. Select the bundle and choose **Actions**, **Delete Bundle**.

4. When prompted for confirmation, choose **Delete Bundle**.

After you delete a custom bundle, you can delete the image you used to create or update the bundle.

To delete an image

1. Open the Amazon WorkSpaces console at https://console.aws.amazon.com/workspaces/.

2. In the navigation pane, choose **Images**.

3. Select the image and choose **Actions**, **Delete Image**.

4. When prompted for confirmation, choose **Delete Image**.

Bring Your Own Windows Desktop Images

If your licensing agreement with Microsoft allows it, you can use your Windows 7 or Windows 10 Enterprise or Professional desktop images for your WorkSpaces. To do this, you must bring your own Microsoft Windows License (BYOL) and provide a Windows 7 or Windows 10 image that meets the requirements listed below. To stay compliant with Microsoft licensing terms, you must run your Amazon WorkSpaces on hardware that is dedicated to you on the AWS cloud. By bringing your own license, you can save money and provide a consistent experience for your users. For more information, see Amazon WorkSpaces Pricing.

Requirements

Before you begin, do the following:

- Review the prerequisites and limitations for importing Windows operating systems from a VM. For more information, see Importing a VM as an Image.
- Verify that your Microsoft licensing agreement allows Windows to be run in a virtual hosted environment.
- Verify that your Windows operating system is 64-bit and activated against your key management servers.
- Verify that your Windows operating system has "English (United States)" as the primary language.
- Verify that your base image contains no additional software beyond what comes with Windows 7 or Windows 10. You can add additional software, like an anti-virus solution, and create a custom image later on.
- Run Sysprep to prepare the image.
- Create the following account with local administrator access before you share the image: WorkSpaces_BYOL. The password for this account will be requested at a later time.
- Verify that the image that you are importing is on a single volume that is smaller than 80 GB, and the format of the image is OVA.
- Amazon WorkSpaces uses a management interface. It's connected to a secure Amazon WorkSpaces management network used for interactive streaming. This allows Amazon WorkSpaces to manage your WorkSpaces. For more information, see Network Interfaces. Confirm that Amazon WorkSpaces can use a /16 range for the management interface in at least one of the following IP ranges:
  - 10.0.0.0/8
  - 100.64.0.0/10
  - 172.16.0.0/12
  - 192.168.0.0/16
  - 198.18.0.0/15
- You must use a minimum of 200 Amazon WorkSpaces in order to run your Amazon WorkSpaces on dedicated hardware. Running your Amazon WorkSpaces on dedicated hardware is necessary to comply with Microsoft licensing requirements.

Getting Started

To get started, contact your AWS account manager or Sales representative, or create a Technical Support case for Amazon WorkSpaces. Your contact will verify whether you have enough dedicated capacity allocated to your account and guide you through BYOL setup.

Monitoring Amazon WorkSpaces

Amazon WorkSpaces and Amazon CloudWatch are integrated, so you can gather and analyze performance metrics. You can monitor these metrics using the CloudWatch console, the CloudWatch command-line interface, or programmatically using the CloudWatch API. CloudWatch also allows you to set alarms when you reach a specified threshold for a metric.

For more information about using CloudWatch and alarms, see the Amazon CloudWatch User Guide.

Prerequisites
To get CloudWatch metrics, enable access on port 443 on the `AMAZON` subset in the `us-east-1` region. For more information, see Port Requirements for Amazon WorkSpaces.

Topics

- Amazon WorkSpaces Metrics
- Dimensions for Amazon WorkSpaces Metrics
- Monitoring Example

Amazon WorkSpaces Metrics

The `AWS/WorkSpaces` namespace includes the following metrics.

Metric	Description	Dimensions	Statistics Available		Units
Available1	The number of WorkSpaces that returned a healthy status.	DirectoryId WorkspaceId	Average, Maximum, imum, Samples	Sum, Min-Data	Count
Unhealthy1	The number of WorkSpaces that returned an unhealthy status.	DirectoryId WorkspaceId	Average, Maximum, imum, Samples	Sum, Min-Data	Count
ConnectionAttempt2	The number of connection attempts.	DirectoryId WorkspaceId	Average, Maximum, imum, Samples	Sum, Min-Data	Count
ConnectionSuccess2	The number of successful connections.	DirectoryId WorkspaceId	Average, Maximum, imum, Samples	Sum, Min-Data	Count
ConnectionFailure2	The number of failed connections.	DirectoryId WorkspaceId	Average, Maximum, imum, Samples	Sum, Min-Data	Count
SessionLaunchTime2	The amount of time it takes to initiate a WorkSpaces session.	DirectoryID WorkspaceID	Average, Maximum, imum, Samples	Sum, Min-Data	Second (time)
InSessionLatency2	The round trip time between the WorkSpaces client and the WorkSpace.	DirectoryID WorkspaceID	Average, Maximum, imum, Samples	Sum, Min-Data	Millisecond (time)

Metric	Description	Dimensions	Statistics Available		Units
SessionDisconnect2	The number of connections that were closed, including user-initiated and failed connections.	DirectoryID WorkspaceID	Average, Maximum, imum, Samples	Sum, Min-Data	Count
UserConnected3	The number of WorkSpaces that have a user connected.	DirectoryID WorkspaceID	Average, Maximum, imum, Samples	Sum, Min-Data	Count
Stopped	The number of WorkSpaces that are stopped.	DirectoryID WorkspaceID	Average, Maximum, imum, Samples	Sum, Min-Data	Count
Maintenance4	The number of WorkSpaces that are under maintenance.	DirectoryID WorkspaceID	Average, Maximum, imum, Samples	Sum, Min-Data	Count

1 Amazon WorkSpaces periodically sends status requests to a WorkSpace. A WorkSpace is marked `Available` when it responds to these requests, and `Unhealthy` when it fails to respond to these requests. These metrics are available at a per-WorkSpace granularity, and also aggregated for all WorkSpaces in an organization.

2 Amazon WorkSpaces records metrics on connections made to each WorkSpace. These metrics are emitted after a user has successfully authenticated via the WorkSpaces client and the client then initiates a session. The metrics are available at a per-WorkSpace granularity, and also aggregated for all WorkSpaces in a directory.

3 Amazon WorkSpaces periodically sends connection status requests to a WorkSpace. Users are reported as connected when they are actively using their sessions. This metric is available at a per-WorkSpace granularity, and is also aggregated for all WorkSpaces in an organization.

4 This metric applies to WorkSpaces that are configured with an AutoStop running mode. If you have maintenance enabled for your WorkSpaces, this metric captures the number of WorkSpaces that are currently under maintenance. This metric is available at a per-WorkSpace granularity, which describes when a WorkSpace went into maintenance and when it was removed.

Dimensions for Amazon WorkSpaces Metrics

Amazon WorkSpaces metrics are available for the following dimensions.

Dimension	Description
DirectoryId	Limits the data you receive to the WorkSpaces in the specified directory. The DirectoryId value is in the form of d-XXXXXXXXXX.
WorkspaceId	Limits the data you receive to the specified WorkSpace. The WorkspaceId value is in the formws-XXXXXXXXXX.

Monitoring Example

The following example demonstrates how you can use the AWS CLI to respond to a CloudWatch alarm and determine which WorkSpaces in a directory have experienced connection failures.

To respond to a CloudWatch alarm

1. Determine which directory the alarm applies to using the describe-alarms command.

```
1  aws cloudwatch describe-alarms --state-value "ALARM"
2
3  {
4    "MetricAlarms": [
5      {
6        ...
7        "Dimensions": [
8          {
9            "Name": "DirectoryId",
10           "Value": "directory_id"
11         }
12       ],
13       ...
14     }
15   ]
16 }
```

2. Get the list of WorkSpaces in the specified directory using the describe-workspaces command.

```
1  aws workspaces describe-workspaces --directory-id directory_id
2
3  {
4    "Workspaces": [
5      {
6        ...
7        "WorkspaceId": "workspace1_id",
8        ...
9      },
10     {
11       ...
12       "WorkspaceId": "workspace2_id",
13       ...
14     },
15     {
16       ...
17       "WorkspaceId": "workspace3_id",
18       ...
19     }
20   ]
21 }
```

3. Get the CloudWatch metrics for each WorkSpace in the directory using the get-metric-statistics command.

```
1  aws cloudwatch get-metric-statistics \
2  --namespace AWS/WorkSpaces \
3  --metric-name ConnectionFailure \
4  --start-time 2015-04-27T00:00:00Z \
5  --end-time 2015-04-28T00:00:00Z \
```

```
 6  --period 3600 \
 7  --statistics Sum \
 8  --dimensions "Name=WorkspaceId,Value=workspace_id"
 9
10  {
11    "Datapoints" : [
12      {
13        "Timestamp": "2015-04-27T00:18:00Z",
14        "Sum": 1.0,
15        "Unit": "Count"
16      },
17      {
18        "Timestamp": "2014-04-27T01:18:00Z",
19        "Sum": 0.0,
20        "Unit": "Count"
21      }
22    ],
23    "Label" : "ConnectionFailure"
24  }
```

Troubleshooting Amazon WorkSpaces Issues

The following information can help you troubleshoot issues with your WorkSpaces.

Topics

- Launching WorkSpaces in my connected directory often fails
- Launching WorkSpaces fails with an internal error
- Can't connect to a WorkSpace with an interactive logon banner
- No WorkSpaces in my directory can connect to the Internet
- I receive a "DNS unavailable" error when I try to connect to my on-premises directory
- I receive a "Connectivity issues detected" error when I try to connect to my on-premises directory
- I receive an "SRV record" error when I try to connect to my on-premises directory
- One of my WorkSpaces has a state of "Unhealthy"
- The state of my apps was not saved when my WorkSpace was stopped

Launching WorkSpaces in my connected directory often fails

Verify that the two DNS servers or domain controllers in your on-premises directory are accessible from each of the subnets that you specified when you connected to your directory. You can verify this connectivity by launching an EC2 instance in each subnet and joining the instance to your directory, using the IP addresses of the two DNS servers.

Launching WorkSpaces fails with an internal error

Check whether your subnets are configured to automatically assign IPv6 addresses to instances launched in the subnet. To check this setting, open the Amazon VPC console, select your subnet, and choose **Subnet Actions, Modify auto-assign IP settings**. If this setting is enabled, you cannot launch WorkSpaces using the Performance or Graphics bundles. Instead, disable this setting and specify IPv6 addresses manually when you launch your instances.

Can't connect to a WorkSpace with an interactive logon banner

Implementing an interactive logon message to display a logon banner prevents users from being able to access their WorkSpaces. The interactive logon message Group Policy setting is not currently supported by Amazon WorkSpaces.

No WorkSpaces in my directory can connect to the Internet

WorkSpaces cannot communicate with the Internet by default. You must explicitly provide Internet access. For more information, see Provide Internet Access from Your WorkSpace.

I receive a "DNS unavailable" error when I try to connect to my on-premises directory

You receive an error message similar to the following when connecting to your on-premises directory:

```
1 DNS unavailable (TCP port 53) for IP: dns-ip-address
```

AD Connector must be able to communicate with your on-premises DNS servers via TCP and UDP over port 53. Verify that your security groups and on-premises firewalls allow TCP and UDP communication over this port.

I receive a "Connectivity issues detected" error when I try to connect to my on-premises directory

You receive an error message similar to the following when connecting to your on-premises directory:

```
1 Connectivity issues detected: LDAP unavailable (TCP port 389) for IP: ip-address
2 Kerberos/authentication unavailable (TCP port 88) for IP: ip-address
3 Please ensure that the listed ports are available and retry the operation.
```

AD Connector must be able to communicate with your on-premises domain controllers via TCP and UDP over the following ports. Verify that your security groups and on-premises firewalls allow TCP and UDP communication over these ports.

- 88 (Kerberos)
- 389 (LDAP)

I receive an "SRV record" error when I try to connect to my on-premises directory

You receive an error message similar to one or more of the following when connecting to your on-premises directory:

```
1 SRV record for LDAP does not exist for IP: dns-ip-address
2
3 SRV record for Kerberos does not exist for IP: dns-ip-address
```

AD Connector needs to obtain the _ldap._tcp.dns-domain-name and _kerberos._tcp.dns-domain-name SRV records when connecting to your directory. You will get this error if the service cannot obtain these records from the DNS servers that you specified when connecting to your directory. Make sure that your DNS servers contains these SRV records. For more information, see SRV Resource Records on Microsoft TechNet.

One of my WorkSpaces has a state of "Unhealthy"

The Amazon WorkSpaces service periodically sends status requests to a WorkSpace. A WorkSpace is marked Unhealthy when it fails to respond to these requests. Common causes for this problem are:

- An application on the WorkSpace is blocking network ports which prevents the WorkSpace from responding to the status request.
- High CPU utilization is preventing the WorkSpace from responding to the status request in a timely manner.
- The computer name of the WorkSpace has been changed. This prevents a secure channel from being established between Amazon WorkSpaces and the WorkSpace.

You can attempt to correct the situation using the following methods:

- Reboot the WorkSpace from the Amazon WorkSpaces console.

- Connect to the unhealthy WorkSpace using the following procedure, which should be used only for troubleshooting purposes:

  1. Connect to an operational WorkSpace in the same directory as the unhealthy WorkSpace.

  2. From the operational WorkSpace, use Remote Desktop Protocol (RDP) to connect to the unhealthy WorkSpace using the IP address of the unhealthy WorkSpace. Depending on the extent of the problem, you might not be able to connect to the unhealthy WorkSpace.

  3. On the unhealthy WorkSpace, confirm that the minimum port requirements are met.

- Rebuild the WorkSpace from the Amazon WorkSpaces console. Because rebuilding a WorkSpace can potentially cause a loss of data, this option should only be used if all other attempts to correct the problem have been unsuccessful.

The state of my apps was not saved when my WorkSpace was stopped

To save the state of your apps, you must have enough free space on the root volume of your WorkSpace to store the total memory offered on the WorkSpace bundle. For example, a Standard Workspace has 4 GB of memory, so you must have 4 GB of free space on the root volume of the WorkSpace.

Also, if the Amazon WorkSpaces service could not communicate with the WorkSpace when a stop request is issued, it will force shut down the operating system and the state of the apps will not be saved.

Amazon WorkSpaces Limits

The following are the limits for Amazon WorkSpaces, per region. To request a limit increase, use the Amazon WorkSpaces Limits form.

Resource	Limit
WorkSpaces	1
Graphics WorkSpaces	0
Images	5

Document History

The following table describes important additions to the Amazon WorkSpaces service and its documentation set. We also update the documentation frequently to address the feedback that you send us.

Change	Description	Date
IP access control groups	You can control the IP addresses from which users can access their WorkSpaces. For more information, see IP Access Control Groups for Your WorkSpaces.	April 30, 2018
In-place upgrades	You can upgrade your Windows 10 BYOL WorkSpaces to a newer version of Windows 10. For more information, see Upgrade Windows 10 BYOL WorkSpaces.	March 9, 2018
Flexible compute options	You can switch your WorkSpaces between the Value, Standard, Performance, and Power bundles. For more information, see Modify a WorkSpace.	December 22, 2017
Configurable storage	You can configure the size of the root and user volumes for your WorkSpaces when you launch them and increase the size of these volumes later on. For more information, see Modify a WorkSpace.	December 22, 2017
Control device access	You can specify the types of devices that have access to WorkSpaces. In addition, you can restrict access to WorkSpaces to trusted devices (also known as managed devices). For more information, see Control Device Access.	June 19, 2017
Inter-forest trusts	You can establish a trust relationship between your AWS Microsoft AD and your on-premises Microsoft Active Directory domain and then provision WorkSpaces for users in the on-premises domain. For more information, see Launch a WorkSpace Using a Trusted Domain.	February 9, 2017
Windows Server 2016 bundles	Amazon WorkSpaces now offers bundles that come with a Windows 10 desktop experience, powered by Windows Server 2016.	November 29, 2016

Change	Description	Date
Web Access	Access your WorkSpaces from a web browser using Amazon WorkSpaces Web Access.	November 18, 2016
Hourly WorkSpaces	You can configure your WorkSpaces so that users are billed by the hour. For more information, see Manage the WorkSpace Running Mode.	August 18, 2016
Windows 10 BYOL	Bring your Windows 10 Desktop License to Amazon WorkSpaces (BYOL).	July 21, 2016
Tagging support	You can now use tags to manage and track your WorkSpaces. For more information, see Tag a WorkSpace.	May 17, 2016
Saved registrations	Every time you enter a new registration code, the WorkSpaces client stores it. This makes it easier to switch between WorkSpaces in different directories or regions.	January 28, 2016
Windows 7 BYOL Chromebook client WorkSpace encryption	Bring your Windows 7 Desktop License to Amazon WorkSpaces (BYOL). Use the Chromebook client. Use WorkSpace encryption (see Encrypt a WorkSpace).	October 1, 2015
CloudWatch monitoring	Added information about CloudWatch monitoring. For more information, see Monitoring Amazon WorkSpaces.	April 28th, 2015
Automatic session reconnect	Added information about the auto session reconnect feature in the WorkSpaces desktop client applications.	March 31st, 2015
Public IP addresses	Added support for automatically assigning a public IP address to your WorkSpaces. For more information, see Configure Automatic IP Addresses.	January 23rd, 2015
Amazon WorkSpaces launched in Asia Pacific (Singapore)	Amazon WorkSpaces is now available in the Asia Pacific (Singapore) region.	January 15th, 2015
Value bundle added Standard bundle updates Office 2013 added	The Value bundle is now available. The Standard bundle hardware has been upgraded. Microsoft Office 2013 is now available in Plus packages.	November 6th, 2014
Image and bundle support	Added support for images and custom bundles. For more information, see WorkSpace Bundles and Images.	October 28th, 2014

Change	Description	Date
PCoIP zero client support	You can now access Amazon WorkSpaces PCoIP zero client devices.	October 15th, 2014
Amazon WorkSpaces launched in Asia Pacific (Tokyo)	Amazon WorkSpaces is now available in the Asia Pacific (Tokyo) region.	August 26th, 2014
Local printer support	Added support for local printers.	August 26th, 2014
Multi-factor authentication	Added support for multi-factor authentication in connected directories.	August 11th, 2014
Default OU support	You can now select a default Organizational Unit (OU) where your WorkSpace machine accounts are placed.	July 7th, 2014
Target domain support	You can now select a separate domain where your WorkSpace machine accounts are created.	July 7th, 2014
Add security group	The ability to add a security group to your WorkSpaces. For more information, see Security Groups for Your WorkSpaces.	July 7th, 2014
Amazon WorkSpaces launched in Asia Pacific (Sydney)	Amazon WorkSpaces is now available in the Asia Pacific (Sydney) region.	May 15th, 2014
Amazon WorkSpaces launched in EU (Ireland)	Amazon WorkSpaces is now available in the EU (Ireland) region.	May 5th, 2014
Public beta	Amazon WorkSpaces is now available as a public beta.	March 25th, 2014

www.ingramcontent.com/pod-product-compliance
Lightning Source LLC
LaVergne TN
LVHW082041050326
832904LV00005B/258